A Poisonous Cocktail?

Aum Shinrikyō's Path to Violence

Ian Reader

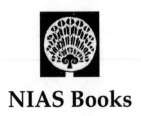

NIAS Books

A POISONOUS COCKTAIL?
Aum Shinrikyō's Path to Violence
by Ian Reader

First published in 1996
Reprinted 1997
by NIAS Publications
Nordic Institute of Asian Studies (NIAS)
Leifsgade 33, 2300 Copenhagen S, Denmark
Tel: (+45) 3154 8844 Fax: (+45) 3296 2530
E-mail: books@nias.ku.dk
Online: http//nias.ku.dk/books/

Typesetting by NIAS
Printed and bound in Great Britain by
Biddles Ltd, Kings Lynn and Guildford

ISBN 87-87062-55-0

Contents

Acknowledgements

The nerve gas attack on the Tokyo subway and the subsequent events relating this attack to a Japanese religious movement, Aum Shinrikyō, have presented those who study Japanese religion in the modern age with the challenge of keeping track of a news story and of a complex affair as it has unfolded, while trying to answer the questions of colleagues and students anxious to learn more about and understand the affair. As an academic working on contemporary Japan, I was driven by my own wish to understand what went on and make some sense of the affair in my own mind, and by the sense of responsibility I felt as a scholar in the field to attempt to answer such questions as best I could. This report is thus intended as a contribution to the broader discussions of the Aum affair that will be necessary in future years. I am aware that, in dealing with so contemporary an event, subsequent information could well affect some of the issues raised in this report. Of necessity, therefore, this is a first stage in more extensive discussions and analyses of the affair and its repercussions which scholars will be making in the years to come.

In dealing with an event that has constantly unfolded as I have been working on it, I have been more dependent than is usually the case on the endeavours and work of colleagues and friends in the field, and here I wish to express my deep gratitude to other scholars who have generously shared their knowledge with me. This report would not have been possible without their help. In this respect I would especially like to thank Robert Kisala, Mark Mullins, Paul Swanson, Shimazono Susumu, Takeda Michio, Richard Young, Trevor Astley and Kashioka Tomihide. I would also like to thank Catherine Wessinger and Mary Maaga, two scholars of new religious movements who have helped me greatly in my understanding of millennialism and of religious violence. I wish also to thank many friends in Japan outside the academic community who collected information and materials for me on the affair. In particular, I wish to thank Kaneko Yoshihiro and Kaneko Ayako, and Sando Takeshi and Sando Minako, who have been such good friends and have provided so much hospitality to my family over the years. In particular I am grateful to them for providing me with some excellent and balanced comments on the affair from the perspective of ordinary Tokyo dwellers.

I would also like to thank the staff at NIAS who have been involved in turning this report into a published item so quickly: Gerald Jackson, for making the encouraging noises that got the project off the ground and for coordinating everything and producing the cover, Liz Bramsen for typing in the corrections, and especially Leena Höskuldsson for her meticulous reading and editing of the text, and for her occasional success in curbing my verbal excesses.

And special thanks to Dorothy, Rosie and Philip Reader for their support and much more besides.

Conventions

All Japanese names are given in standard Japanese form, with family name first followed by given name.

Erratum

The title *Hi izuri kuni saiwai chikashi* that appears on pp. 56, 63 and 113 should read *Hi izuri kuni, wazawai chikashi.*

About the the Author

Ian Reader is Senior Research Fellow at the Nordic Institute of Asian Studies, and also a member of the Department of Japanese Studies at the University of Stirling in Scotland. His main publications include *Religion in Contemporary Japan* (1991) and *Pilgrimage in Popular Culture* (ed. with Tony Walter, 1993).

Introduction

Although there have been a number of cases of terrorism by extremist political groups in post-war Japan, and although religious violence and conflict are by no means unknown there, the poison gas attack on the Tokyo subway on March 20 1995, which killed 12 people and injured thousands of others, appeared to represent something new in Japan, a case of indiscriminate terrorism by a religious movement. Immediately after the attack suspicions fell upon a new religious movement, Aum Shinrikyō which, despite being only a decade or so old and rather small by Japanese standards (it was founded in the 1980s and had around 10,000 followers in Japan in 1995), had already become widely known in Japan due to its often controversial and high profile activities. Aum[1] had attracted much attention, and indeed notoriety, in previous years, due, inter alia, to its campaigns for support (which included the formation of its own political party and a widely reported political campaign in 1990), and because it was a world-rejecting movement which had built communes in a number of places in Japan, coming into conflict as a result with local communities in the areas where it established communes, and with the families of those who had dropped out of society to join it. It had often clashed with the media and had been the subject of various media attacks and journalistic enquiries and exposés which sought to paint it as a dangerous and disruptive religious movement.[2]

---

1. In this report I shall refer to the movement as Aum rather than the longer Aum Shinrikyō, for the sake of brevity.
2. The first exposé of Aum was done in 1989 by the *Sunday Mainichi* magazine (see below, Chapter 2). A good example of a journalistic account of Aum which portrayed it as dangerous and that was especially critical of Asahara Shōkō was that by Egawa Shōko (1995, first published in 1991): Egawa has published other articles and books about Aum as well.

Its founder and leader Asahara Shōkō was not only a highly recognisable figure due to his long hair, beard and Indian-style clothes, but also an extremely controversial one due to his apparent power over his followers and the demands made on them by his religion. He had also achieved prominence because of his frequent, drastic prophecies, which stated that an apocalypse would occur before the end of the century to engulf the vast majority of humanity and sweep away the corrupt material world and destroy Japanese society. He proclaimed that he was a messiah who had come to save his followers from the apocalypse and lead them forward to form a new, ideal spiritual universe that would emerge from the ruins of the old. Asahara's apocalyptic visions were also reinforced by his recurrent allegations that various forces in Japan were engaged in a conspiracy to destroy Aum.

Police Raids on Aum

Aum was thus already known as a conflictual and controversial religious movement before March 1995. Indeed, several allegations had been made against it in the media and elsewhere in the past accusing it of complicity in a number of acts of violence, including the kidnappings of people who came into conflict with it, the disappearance of a lawyer, who was involved in a dispute with Aum, and his family in 1989, and one earlier case of sarin gas poisonings in the town of Matsumoto in central Japan on June 27 1994. A small number of Aum members had been implicated in the kidnapping of Kariya Kiyoshi, a property dealer who had been in dispute with Aum, from a Tokyo street on February 28 1995: the rental van used in the kidnapping had been linked to an Aum member, and through him to the movement's headquarters at Kamikuishiki, a rural area near Mount Fuji in Yamanashi prefecture, about one hundred miles from Tokyo. Early on the morning of March 22 – just two days after the Tokyo sarin attack – massive raids were conducted at Kamikuishiki and at other of Aum's premises throughout Japan, ostensibly under a warrant seeking the whereabouts of Kariya.[3] Although he was not found in these raids, evidence was uncovered that he had been abducted by the movement, and subsequently various members have confessed to kidnapping and killing him, and disposing of his body in an

3.   It has been suggested in some quarters that the raids may have been planned before the March 20 sarin attack, not just in connection with the Kariya case but with the earlier poison gas attack at Matsumoto. See Shimosato 1995: 239, and also see the comments on this issue in Chapter 4, below.

industrial microwave oven owned by Aum. The raids, which were covered in depth by the mass media, clearly showed that in the view of the authorities, Aum was behind the Tokyo sarin attack and instilled in the minds of all those who witnessed them on Japanese television the notion that Aum was dangerous, for the police and the back-up forces carrying them out wore camou-flaged battle fatigues and gas masks, while some also carried caged canaries to serve as a warning against poisonous gases.

The raids turned up large quantities of chemicals and other materials linking the movement to the attack, and also brought to public notice a number of facilities that Aum had built (some of them covertly) at Kamikuishiki, including laboratories, where it was, according to subsequent charges, manufacturing chemicals and illegal drugs.[4] Evidence was also found, in these and subsequent raids, of schemes to produce weapons, including guns, and of highly speculative plans to develop various chemical and biological weapons, as well as other weapons of mass destruction. Although nothing concrete was substantiated at the time, there were reports (based on the contents of notebooks and computer disks belonging to Aum activists later implicated in other of its illegal activities) that the movement had been planning various large-scale attacks in Japan when they were apprehended. It has been alleged, for example, that Aum had plans to carry out even greater atrocities, such as spraying sarin gas over Tokyo from a helicopter, in a concerted attempt to destabilise Japan, cause mass destruction and bring about the events that, in Aum's apocalyptic vision, would lead to Armageddon, the final war which was a necessary step before the realisation of the millennium it preached was imminent.[5]

Besides these materials, the raids also uncovered a vast amount of money in ready cash, as well as a stockpile of gold, which were widely assumed to have been gathered in order to finance a campaign against the wider world. These monetary finds also, especially when coupled with the 10 million yen in cash

---

4. The laboratories were concealed behind or beneath various Aum facilities devoted to religious worship, including a temple which enshrined a statue of the Hindu deity Shiva, who was widely venerated in Aum.

5. The plan to spray gas over Tokyo was first reported in one of Japan's more sensationalist magazines, *Focus*, but later was reported by several more mainstream newspapers and has since been given wide currency. There are some circumstantial facts that could be read as verifying this plan, for Aum had acquired a Russian helicopter capable of carrying large payloads, and a leading Aum member had trained as a helicopter pilot in the USA (see below, Chapter 4).

found on Asahara when he was arrested, and with the emerging stories of how Aum pressurised its members to make large donations to the movement, contributed to a series of media horror stories, in which Aum came to be depicted not merely as a dangerous and violent movement, but as one that was venal and grasping, and that exploited its own members.

As a result of these and subsequent and continuing raids on Aum premises and the evidence they uncovered, along with the growing series of media articles, a general consensus developed in Japan that the movement in general (and in particular its leader, Asahara) was behind the Tokyo sarin attack and various other cases of violence. The images that were transmitted through the media suggested that the movement was not only involved in attacking external targets, however. Viewers saw footage of emaciated and sometimes comatose Aum members who had been engaged in extreme austerities, being led away to hospitals, of children who were allegedly malnourished and who had been kept apart from their parents, and of other Aum members at Kamikuishiki wearing special PSI (Perfect Salvation Initiation) units. These were items of electronic headgear produced by Aum's science and technology department in 1994 and designed to put the disciple on the same wavelength as Asahara. Members rented them for a month at a time, and wore them constantly, thus cutting out all external stimuli and allowing themselves, so it was believed, to exist solely in harmony with their spiritual master and leader. This provided some of the most dramatic and frightening images of the whole affair, for what came across on television screens were images of apparently zombie-like followers wearing their strange headgear, estranged from the ordinary realities of the world and looking every bit as if (to use a popular but highly contentious term) they had been 'brainwashed'.[6]

These images, like much of the media coverage, which verged (especially in the earlier months of the affair) on the sensational, contained partial truths and partial misrepresentations. For instance, Aum members did engage in extreme austerities and led spartan

---

6. The notion that some new religions 'brainwash' their members has been widely promoted by the mass-media, particularly in the 1970s and 1980s. The term remains popular in the media even though academic specialists on new religious movements have generally refuted the idea that 'brainwashing' can explain why people join such movements (see, for example, Barker 1984, esp. pp. 121–148). Other, more structured and less emotive discussions of what leads people into extraordinarily deep levels of commitment and belief exist as well (see, for example, Lifton 1961).

lives which made them emaciated, but as a rule they did this voluntarily. However, there was also a certain amount of ill-treatment of members, and the movement had a record of detaining, against their will, members who wished to leave: indeed, in recent months numerous criminal charges have been laid against senior Aum members in this regard. The 'Aum children', mentioned above, had been placed in the movement's care by members who, when they renounced the world to live in Aum communes, ceased to have direct contact with their children and left them to the movement to bring up and educate. The education they received would not, however, have satisfied normal conventions.

The Arrests

Although Aum spokespeople vigorously denied all the charges against the movement at first, gradually the denials weakened as increasing numbers of leading figures in the movement were arrested and charged with various crimes, and as reports of the confessions they were making in custody began to be filtered out by the police to the media. By the end of 1995 several of the leading personnel in Aum had appeared in court and had admitted various charges such as manufacturing sarin and releasing it on the subway (see below, Chapter 4).

Asahara, however, remained at large for some weeks after the raids, amidst massive speculation as to his whereabouts. Eventually he was arrested on May 16, at Aum's Kamikuishiki headquarters. Police broke into one of its buildings and found him hiding in a small, concealed room where he was found, according to reports, in possession of a large amount of money in cash.[7] Subsequently Asahara has been charged with a number of crimes, including murder and conspiracy to murder. His trial was originally scheduled to start on October 26 1995 but, largely because he fired his defence counsel just before it began, thus giving no time for alternative counsel to be adequately briefed in

---

7.   Although there was an apparent nation-wide manhunt for Asahara from March 22 until the day of his arrest (and numerous reports of sightings of him and his family in various places), it appears that he was at Kamikuishiki all the while. It is also probable that the police knew where he was, but were waiting until they had been able to arrest various other people involved in the attacks first (particularly Inoue Yoshihiro, widely considered one of the main protagonists in Aum's illicit activities, who was finally caught, after a nation-wide search, a couple of days before the police moved on Asahara) and had been able to collect enough evidence to directly tie Asahara to the attacks.

time, this had to be postponed and is now scheduled to start in April 1996.[8]

The affair has extended far beyond the immediate issues of the Tokyo and Matsumoto murders, and the schemes to create various illegal weapons. Charges have been levelled against various Aum members relating also to earlier activities, such as the murder of the lawyer and his family mentioned above, the illegal detention of people who were seeking to leave the movement, the extortion of funds from reluctant members and their families, and various charges related to Aum's purchase of tracts of land on which to build its communes. In all, well over one hundred people in Aum, including much of its hierarchy, have been charged with offences. The more serious charges, against those alleged to be most directly involved in the sarin attacks and other murders, could carry the death penalty, and these in particular could lead to long and complex trials. The Japanese legal system works rather slowly and it has been generally assumed that the main trials, especially that of Asahara (who is being tried separately from his alleged co-conspirators)[9] may take several years to be finalised.

Despite the case being still sub-judice, all discussions of the case, whether in the mass media or in the various books and articles produced by scholars so far,[10] have operated on the basic

---

8. Subsequently Asahara has re-engaged this same counsel, and the courts have appointed a number of back-up counsels to prevent further delays. Under Japanese law, defendants charged with serious crimes that could result in long imprisonment or the death penalty have to be represented by legal counsel who have been thoroughly briefed in the case. Thus it was impossible to immediately replace Asahara's counsel with a court-appointed one.

9. The reasons stated for trying him separately are that he is believed to have a powerful influence over the others, and that his presence in court might make his former colleagues reluctant to confess to the crimes, as they have apparently done to the police. In addition, while most of the others involved have made confessions, Asahara has not, and the case against him rests very much on what the other accused say. These are more likely to avoid the ultimate penalty if they are able to convince the court that they operated under his influence, a theme that has characterised the procedures that have so far emerged.

10. There have been numerous books and articles, mostly journalistic, but with a growing number of more academic works, in Japanese, and a small number of academic papers in English. All commence from the common assumption that Aum's leaders are guilty as charged, an assumption that appears to be substantiated by reports of the confessions made by many of those involved. See for example Inoue et. al., Fujita, Shimazono and Yamaori, and in English Kisala, Young, Mullins, and Hardacre (all 1995).

assumption that a number of people in the upper echelons of Aum Shinrikyō, including Asahara, are guilty of the charges made against them, including the sarin attacks. At present, the number of killings attributed to Aum is 25. A dissident member named Taguchi Shūji was killed, it appears, at Aum's headquarters in February 1989. The three members of the Sakamoto family (the lawyer mentioned above, and his wife and baby son) were also killed in 1989. Another member, Ochida Kōtarō, who fell out with the movement, was killed at Aum's headquarters in February 1994. Seven people died in the Matsumoto sarin attack, and the property dealer Kariya Kiyoshi was kidnapped and murdered, as mentioned above. Finally, twelve people were killed in the Tokyo subway attack. There have also been numerous suggestions and hints that more dissident members may have been disposed of secretly at Aum facilities.

Besides the killings, thousands have been injured, some permanently, in the mass poisonings. In addition, a succession of further violent incidents following on from the Tokyo attack and the raids in spring in 1995 have been attributed to Aum (and in some cases have subsequently been admitted by Aum members), including the attempted assassination of the Head of Japan's National Police Agency, the bomb mailed to the Tokyo Governor's office on the day of Asahara's arrest, which seriously injured an aide, and a series of other attacks using poisonous gases on trains and stations in the Tokyo-Yokohama area. Members of Aum have also been on the receiving end of violence, and one of its most prominent members, Murai Hideo, who was in charge of Aum's science and technology programme (and who was widely believed to be closely involved in the production of sarin), was stabbed to death in public by a man with gangster connections, apparently in retribution for the sarin attack, on April 23 1995.[11]

It is recognised that those directly involved in the 'Aum affair' are only a small (though highly placed) number of the movement's members, and that most Aum members were

---

11. The attacker has subsequently pleaded guilty and been sentenced to 12 years' imprisonment, while the person who is alleged to have ordered the attack, and who also has gangster affiliations, is due to stand trial. The motives behind the attacks remain unclear at present, although the perpetrators were seemingly enraged at what they saw as Murai's guilt in the poisonings.

unaware of what was being carried out by their leaders. The movement has, nonetheless, been ordered to disband by the government under the terms of the 1952 Subversive Activities Prevention Law, a process that will strip Aum of its remaining assets, which will be used to compensate victims of its attacks. The movement will be prohibited from operating as an organisation after this, although members may continue to practice their faith as individuals.

Perspectives on the Aum Affair

Much of the information on the case so far has come from media sources and disseminated through a media filter. This makes it not always so easy to sort out how much of what has been reported is true, and how much has been sensationalised. There are, however, other sources of information that can be used in helping reconstruct the way that events developed in Aum. In particular there is a fairly large corpus of publications by Aum available, including numerous volumes of Asahara's sermons and discussions of Aum's affairs. Through these we can trace Aum's development and the ways in which Asahara's thoughts have evolved, and can discern some clues as to why Aum became engaged in violent activities, and can link some of the events that took place with the changes in Aum's thinking. Eventually it is possible that more detailed materials (e.g., the documents and transcripts from the trials when they are over, and from the police investigations) might become available, but it may be many years before any detailed and balanced analysis can be written that is not influenced by the traumas of the present.[12]

However, it is important that some attempts are made to examine the case at present and to start providing some tentative answers to the question of why Aum Shinrikyō, a seemingly idealistic new religion which preached the virtues of asceticism

---

12. The case of Jonestown (1978) may provide a parallel case: in its aftermath there were numerous academic and journalistic accounts and explanations of the affair yet it is perhaps only very recently, with the work of Mary Maaga (1995) that we are really beginning to understand the processes that led the people at Jonestown to accept suicide. In Japan, the work by Patricia G. Steinhoff (1992) on the Rengō Sekigun affair (the internal violence in a Japanese Red Army political group in 1972, in which 12 of the group were killed by their colleagues) has benefited from being able to use the court transcripts and the diaries and writings of some of the survivors. Steinhoff was also able to conduct interviews with some of the participants in prison.

and renunciation, became a murderous movement. It is from this perspective that this report has been written.

Its aim is to give some details of the affair as it unfolded, to detail the confluence of events and influences that intensified Aum's dystopic perceptions of the world and increased its antipathetic attitude to Japanese society, and to present an analysis of the factors which, in my view, led Aum to become involved in violence. How did Aum, in the words of a former member, come to be, by 1994, on a 'war footing'? What caused it to develop what a prominent member and 'minister' in Aum's alternative government organisation (formed in 1994: see Chapter 4, below), Noda Naruhito, has recently called a 'persecution complex' (*higai mōsō*) which, especially from 1993 onwards, clouded or coloured all its actions?[13] How did Aum get to the point when, in the views expressed by Asahara Shōkō especially from 1993 onwards, it saw itself as being attacked by a conspiracy of devious forces including the American air force, the Japanese government, the Jews, the Freemasons, the Japanese Imperial family and even popular American entertainers living in Japan, so that it felt forced to strike out against the society that was oppressing it before it itself was crushed?

In this report, I shall draw attention to some aspects of Aum's history and to some of its characteristics, such as its communal and hierarchic nature, its focus on world-rejection as a religious act (in which members became renunciates, cut ties with their families and ceased virtually all interaction with anyone save those in the immediate hierarchy and with Asahara), and the charismatic authority of Asahara Shōkō and his prophetic utterances, which eventually painted Aum into a corner and increased its need for dramatic events and disasters to verify his teachings. I shall also draw attention to Aum's millennialist views, which became increasingly pessimistic and dramatic between 1986 and 1995, its sense of mission and its apparent sense of failure to fully carry this out, its repeated conflicts with mainstream society, its growing sense that it was being rejected and, subsequently, persecuted, by that society, and the increasing

---

13. *Shūkan Asahi* Oct. 13, 1995: 25. Noda, according to the *Shūkan Asahi* magazine, has become Aum's *de facto* leader and spokesman following the arrest in October 1995 of Jōyu Fumihiro (who had acted as spokesman and leader for the movement from March to October) on charges of persuading others to make false statements about Aum's land purchases.

expressions of fear and paranoia that arose within Aum as a result. Linked to all these strands – and a crucial ingredient in the cocktail – was Aum's and Asahara's predilection for sensational events, self-publicity and drama, all of which served to bring Aum into public attention. This manifested itself not only in the dramas of the Tokyo subway, but in the frequent demonstrations Aum put on for the media of its members' apparent spiritual prowess, the various forays Aum made into the media and into politics, and the strident and attention-grabbing focus of the books it published, which bore titles like *Doomsday* and were full of dramatic predictions about the fate of the world, and wild accusations of attacks on Aum. All of these together served to produce in Aum (or at least in its upper echelons) a disastrous mixture in which estrangement from basic realities was coupled with contempt and arrogance for the outside world, and fuelled by a paranoia produced from a millennialist mind-set coupled with a growing sense of failure to achieve its own mission.

The Structure of this Report

This report is, where possible, historical in structure, in that I discuss Aum from its very earliest beginnings (in Chapter 1) through to the events of March 1995 (in Chapter 4). In some places, however, it has been necessary to move a little ahead of the historical sequence in order to show how certain facets of Aum's teaching and nature (e.g. its intense focus on asceticism, which is discussed in Chapter 1) led to later critical events. In Chapter 1 I shall give a brief outline of Aum's early history, discussing Aum's and Asahara's roots, outlining the religious influences behind the movement and the background from which it and its leader emerged. In Chapter 2 I shall continue to examine Aum's history, but with particular reference to the crucial period of (approximately) April 1989 to April 1990, in which Aum began to get embroiled in disputes with the outside world and to commit violent acts. In Chapter 2 I shall also discuss some of the tensions that started to emerge in the movement. In particular, I shall look at the relative lack of success Aum had in recruiting large numbers of followers, as well as examining some of the problems that arose between Aum and the communities in the areas where it began to build its communes.

In Chapter 3, I shall continue the discussion of Aum's development particularly through examining some of Asahara's sermons and publications in the period between 1992 and 1995, showing how these represent an escalating sense of despair with, and hostility to, the outside world, and how they illustrate the growing conviction in Aum that Armageddon is imminent. In Chapter 3 I shall also show how Aum's 'persecution complex' developed, leading it to feel the necessity of going onto a war footing against society. In Chapter 4 I shall outline the practical process through which Aum prepared for the war it felt, because of its leader's prophecies, was imminent, showing how Aum developed an alternative government structure, how it set about arming itself, how it finally used its weapons, and how it came to be the chief suspect in the Tokyo subway affair.

Chapter 4 is intended to bring the affair up to date as it has evolved so far (as of early 1996). In the Conclusion I shall attempt to go beyond the discussion of data in these chapters, to presenting a brief overview of some of the repercussions of the affair so far in Japan, along with an analysis of what I see as the primary factors in the affair. I shall also attempt to draw some parallels with two other movements, one the Japanese political terrorist group Rengō Sekigun, which was involved in violent activities in Japan in the 1960s and 1970s, and which imploded with great internal violence in 1972, and the other another communally based religious movement, the Rajneesh movement, which became involved in conflicts with the communities around its commune in Oregon, the USA, and many of whose leaders were eventually charged with criminal activities, including poisoning their enemies. These two comparative cases shed some light on the social and religious dynamics of the Aum case and suggest that what happened with Aum should not be seen as an entirely unique event but one that has some parallels and points of reference both from the Japanese social perspective and from the perspective of the comparative study of religion.

Chapter 1

Asahara Shōkō and the Roots of Aum Shinrikyō

Aum and the 'new' new religions

Aum Shinrikyō's development is so closely interwoven with the life and utterances of its leader Asahara Shōkō that the two cannot be separated, and accordingly this outline of the religion's history and its basic teachings is also an account of Asahara's life up to 1995.[1] Aum was one of a number of new religious movements known by the collective term 'new new religions' (*shin shin shūkyō*) that either developed or came into prominence in the 1980s in Japan.[2] Although some of its characteristics (including its extreme asceticism and communal nature) are rather unique, Aum also shared several of the characteristics commonly ascribed to these religions and was (at least until recent events caused it to be placed in a separate and unique category of its own) often discussed academically and in the media as an example of this religious phenomenon, which in

---

1. I am aware that others who attained high positions of leadership in Aum also played a part in the development of the religion and its teachings, and that they may well have played a more active role in the affair than has so far been discussed in reports of it (for further comments on this issue, see below, Conclusion). Asahara has apparently stated in testimony to his interrogators that other senior figures in the movement had taken a lead in its activities independent of him and outside of his knowledge (*Asahi Shinbun* Oct. 5 1995). However, he may well be saying such things in order to deflect some of the blame for the killings away from himself: the fact remains that his teachings were at the centre of Aum's development and that he remains, as far as one can discern, the central force in the movement.
2. For a general overview of these religions see Reader 1991 and Shimazono 1992.

many respects characterises many of the dynamics of late-twentieth century Japanese religion. The rise of the 'new' new religions in general has been linked also to the growth of interest, especially among urban, educated Japanese youth, in occult phenomena and the possibilities of acquiring supernatural powers. These religions have been seen also as expressing a reaction to the increasing rationalisation of the age and against scientific materialism, and as reflecting the increasing dissatisfactions of modern people with the apparent spiritual desolation of a modern society that appears capable of inflicting increasing levels of stress and hard work on its members compensated only by material rewards, which themselves are tenuous and at the risk of economic downturns and recessions (such, indeed, as Japan has suffered in the 1990s).

In reflecting the sentiment that modern society has lost its way, and that therefore new paradigms are needed to cope with the demands of modernity, the 'new' new religions have frequently also espoused millennialist themes, suggesting that the current world is heading towards a disaster caused by its spiritual failure: in particular this sense of imminent disaster has been underpinned by fears and concerns about the threat of nuclear war or of an ecological crisis, both of which symbolise the ways in which science and technology have been misused and have led the world astray. The 'new' new religions have also tended to see this apparent disaster as heralding the end of a civilisation based on scientific materialism, and the birth of a new age in which a better, more spiritually advanced, compassionate and utopian world will be established. Whilst not all of the 'new' new religions speak in such terms, this has been a prevalent theme of many, and the general concept of a shift in paradigms has become a powerful religious theme in the latter part of this century. How the shift will occur varies: some 'new' new religions suggest that they will save the world from the coming crisis through their own spiritual powers and those of their leader (i.e. they will bring about a spiritual revolution before the millennium, and that the transition will be accomplished peacefully). Others have inclined towards the notion of catastrophic millennialism – the idea that the millennium will be preceded by cataclysms and destruction that are, in fact, necessary in order to bring about the coming of the new age and of a better, more spiritually advanced world. Unsurprisingly, whichever stance has been taken on what will precede the coming of the millennium, the religions that have been most concerned with it have, naturally, portrayed themselves and their leaders as being at the forefront of the new age.

The end of the calendrical millennium has been widely seen as the temporal focus of this turning point. The notion that the end of the century is going to be the time of reckoning, as it were, for the world has been strongly reinforced by the predictions of Nostradamus, which have attracted immense interest in Japan as a result of the popular translations of them into Japanese by Goshima Tsutomu in 1973. The prophecies of Nostradamus have become widely read and utilised among the 'new' new religions not only because they appear to predict cataclysms in 1999 but also because they seem, at least in their Japanese translation, to suggest that a spiritual saviour will come from the East to save the world. Not surprisingly, many of the religious leaders who follow a millennialist line in Japan (including Asahara) have identified themselves with this saviour, and have read into Nostradamus' work a prediction of their own coming.[3]

While Aum was of a catastrophic millennialist bent, it had in its initial stages of development been far more optimistic, stating that the threatened cataclysm could be avoided and the millennium achieved without disaster through its spiritual actions and through Asahara's leadership. However, as we shall see, the closer the temporal millennium came, the more pessimistic Asahara's views of averting catastrophe became, and the less possible he saw it that all humanity could be saved and led forward to the new world until, ultimately, only Aum's highly trained practitioners were seen as spiritually capable and worthy of survival in the final war, Armageddon, that would come before the millennium. This progressively pessimistic view of the extent of the damage that would occur, and indeed be necessary, before the new world could emerge, was paralleled by Aum's view of the material world and of those who lived in it, who came to be seen

---

3.   On the influence of Nostradamus in Japanese religion see Shimada 1995: 103–116. Interestingly, Asahara was especially concerned at some of the oblique textual references in Nostradamus' work, and displayed a greater critical faculty than several other Japanese new religious leaders, who took the (sometimes inaccurate) Japanese translations as gospel and did not look closely into their meanings, rather taking what they wanted out of the texts. Asahara, by contrast, was concerned to have the texts accurately interpreted and thus he established an Aum translation team to study the language of the original and to go to France to conduct research on the texts themselves (Shimada 1995: 116–117).

as inimical to the salvationist message of hope the movement offered. This negative view of the outside world and the increasingly pessimistic view of the nature of the apocalypse that would afflict it were accompanied by growing degrees of conflict between Aum and the outside world, and they thus also played a major part in intensifying the movement's general attitudes. These issues will be discussed more fully later.

Like many of the 'new' new religions, Aum was highly eclectic in nature. These movements have generally drawn on a mixture of themes and ideas from a variety of religious sources, ranging from the Japanese folk religious tradition, to Buddhism, Shinto and Christianity, along with an infusion of occultist and New Age ideas. Aum was little different in displaying a similar eclecticism, which was based in Asahara's own readings and experiences, and on ideas and techniques that attracted his interest or which he felt could be usefully employed by his followers.

The name of the religion is itself a mixture of Indian and Japanese themes: *Aum* comes from Sanskrit and refers to the powers of destruction and creation in the universe, while the Japanese *Shinrikyō* means 'teaching of supreme truth'. Aum particularly utilised aspects of Hindu and esoteric Buddhist cosmology and practice: the concept of a path towards higher consciousness via a variety of stages marked by various initiations which form a crucial ritual practice; the importance of the spiritual leader or guru as guide and as the source of initiation; and the importance of ascetic practices – yoga, meditation, and renunciation of the world. It also expressed various aspects of contemporary Japanese religion as mentioned above, such as millennialism allied to a strong critique and, ultimately, rejection of contemporary materialism, along with a deep reverence for the charismatic powers of its leader and his ability to guide followers to the enlightenment.

The mixture of Indian and Japanese motifs in Aum extended also to its focuses of worship (which included the Hindu deity Shiva), the clothing and bearing of its leader, and the Indian initiatory names given to Aum members. Asahara's robes and flowing hair and beard, which made him instantly recognisable and which were a prominent feature of Aum posters seeking to catch the attention of passers-by, are more reminiscent of Indian religious leaders than of Japanese new religious leaders, who tend to reaffirm their Japanese identity through the use of Japanese clothes (e.g. Kiriyama Seiyū of Agonshū, who dresses in Japanese Buddhist robes or in the clothes of a *yamabushi* or Japanese mountain ascetic). I think it is significant that Aum chose to highlight Indian forms in this way, since it implies a basic rejection of Japanese matters: unlike some of the 'new' new religions such as Kōfuku no Kagaku and Agonshū, whose millennialism is allied to a strong sense of Japanese identity in which Japan is seen as the spiritual centre from which world salvation will come in the time of crisis, Aum displays hardly any nationalistic leanings: indeed, Japanese society increasingly came to be seen as an oppressive force that first rejected and then sought to crush Asahara's movement, and as a primary obstruction that had to be destroyed before the millennium could come about.

Among the Hindu motifs and practices that attained high prominence in Aum was that of yoga, accompanied by a focus on physical and spiritual austerities which were seen as bestowing extraordinary physical powers on their practitioners. Aum also had strong leanings towards Buddhism. Its cosmology, practices and imagery were broadly based on its understandings and interpretations of Buddhism, incorporated many Buddhist ideas, and utilised Buddhist terminology.[4] Such notions as those of transmigration and rebirth, that this world is basically sinful and concerned with suffering, and that a path exists out of that suffering, through spiritual disciplines such as world renunciation and meditation, towards better rebirths and enlightenment, are based on Buddhist ideas. Buddhist names and terms from Sanskrit were used for Aum publications (it published magazines called *Mahāyāna* and *Vajrayāna Sacca)* and shifts in its teaching were legitimated or interpreted as movements along a progressive path towards higher forms of religion, with the shift in Aum's focus from being a Mahāyāna to a Vajrayāna Buddhist movement (which occurred in 1990) being seen as a step in this

---

4. One should note here that although the interpretations made by Asahara could often be seen as misrepresentations of Buddhism (e.g. the apparent legitimation he found in Vajrayāna Buddhist texts for taking the lives of 'less spiritually advanced' beings so as to help them to a better rebirth), and although Buddhist scholars have been quick to argue that Aum was not and should not be considered as 'Buddhist', this is how the movement generally defined and saw itself.

progression.[5] In particular Aum emphasised its use and command of esoteric and tantric Buddhist practices, which were accessed by its leader and which were transmitted directly to his followers through various initiation rituals, which (as will be seen later) themselves became the focus of much controversy.[6]

Aum also had a particular fondness for Tibetan Buddhist ideas and imagery: not only did Asahara have himself photographed with the Dalai Lama and make great use of this apparent association with the Tibetan leader,[7] but Tibetan words and concepts, particularly the Tibetan idea of the *bardo*, the 49-day period of transmigration after death when it is believed that the spirit can be guided to a better rebirth, became central to Aum. Aum's concept of *poa* – the transference of consciousness from the living to the dead, so as to enable the dead to attain a higher rebirth than they would have otherwise merited – is closely linked to this notion and has similar derivations: in Aum's usage this concept came to imply that the spiritually advanced could enhance the lot after death of the spiritually backward. Through the *poa* rituals the family of the dead person, too, was considered to become more closely connected to Aum.[8]

Besides these Hindu and Buddhist elements, Aum also added a mixture of Christian images into its worldview. Asahara's

5.   Again one should note that this idea that there is a progressive path in Buddhism, in which the Vajrayana superceded the Mahāyāna path, is an Aum interpretation and reading of the matter.

6.   See Reader 1994 for a discussion of how the image of esoteric Buddhism has long been utilised in Japanese religion to further claims of religious power and legitimation, and how it has specifically been used in Agonshū (a movement in which Asahara studied for some time). The affirmation of Aum's tantric leanings can be found in numerous Aum publications (see, e.g. Aum Shinrikyō (ed) n.d. *Shugyō* p. 3.

7.   The Dalai Lama had met Asahara (as he had many other Japanese religious leaders), been photographed with him and exchanged compliments through formal letters. These items (the letters and photographs) have since been utilised by Aum to construct the image of a close and approving relationship (since refuted by the Dalai Lama, who has pointed out that such violent activities as Aum has been accused of are contrary to Buddhist teaching). This pattern, of using foreign religious leaders so as to enhance one's own image and religious status is very common in Japan, with the Pope and the Dalai Lama being the two most targeted religious leaders.

8.   See Aum Translation Committee (ed) (1992) p. 156 (where the term is transcribed as Pho-wa) and Aum Shinrikyō (ed) n.d. *Shugyō* pp. 16–17 for descriptions of this practice, which in many respects is not dissimilar to traditional Japanese ancestral practices, where the beneficial situation of the spirit who has been aided by its kin's actions on its behalf translates into increased happiness for the kin themselves.

millennialist perspectives were influenced by his readings of the Revelations of St. John (which apparently he started to read in about 1988) and its discussions of the Apocalypse. His usage of the term and concept of Armageddon as the final war when mass destruction would sweep away the perfidies of this world came from his biblical readings. These revelatory and prophetic aspects of the Bible coloured many of his own prophecies, while illustrations of biblical images such as the Four Horsemen of the Apocalypse found their way into various of his books. Besides being the saviour foretold by Nostradamus, he also identified himself as the Christ (most notably in his two-volume series *Kirisuto Sengen*, translated as *Declaring Myself the Christ*),[9] who had come to save the world or, as he also at times prophesied, to be sacrificed in order that the world might be saved.[10]

Asahara Shōkō and the Foundations of Aum Shinrikyō

That the rather ad hoc mixture of religious influences and ideas described above could hold together required a focal point of authority and inspiration, and this of course was provided, as is normal in the new religions of Japan, by the charismatic figure of its leader. Asahara's life and background are thus of much interest and, in the aftermath of the affair, of some often sensationalised media speculation.

Since the Aum affair became public, Asahara has been effectively demonised in the media, with numerous negative stories about him as a child, which thus seek to explain the affair as a projection of his 'evil' personality, and to construct a psychological profile depicting him as an embittered youth at war with Japanese society from early on. This process of demonisation has encouraged those who were acquainted with him in his childhood to provide stories that underpin these instant analyses and portray him as an ambitious bully. Whilst one might expect the media to produce such images, they also cloud any realistic analysis of his early life before he became a public figure. There

---

9.   The first volume of the Japanese version was published in 1991 and the second in 1992: an English translation came out also in 1992.

10. Although this sacrifical image is found in *Declaring Myself the Christ* it is not as prominent in later Asahara publications such as those discussed in Chapter 3: like his brief flirtations with and musings about suicide it would appear that this sacrificial motif and inclination was less powerful than the drive to impose a solution on the world.

has been a lot of speculative psychologising that his childhood background provides reasons for his subsequent behaviour. Thus he has been 'analysed' as having an inferiority complex due to his deprived background, childhood poverty, low social status and blindness, coupled with a frustration and rage at the tensions between his burning ambitions and his failures to advance in the education world. All of these have been widely explained as leading to 'overcompensation', i.e. being driven to develop his authority over others, especially of a higher educational background, being obsessed with accumulating money to compensate for his poverty, and perhaps being consumed with anger against society at large because of his disability and his low social status.[11]

As yet, however, we have no serious or in-depth psychological profile of Asahara (although no doubt in time this will become available) and until such time it is impossible to determine how far his early background affected the later development of his teachings or of his religious activities.[12] Thus I shall attempt here to keep to the basic facts that are commonly known about Asahara's past.

He was born in Kumamoto prefecture in the southern island of Kyūshū in 1955, the fourth son (out of seven children in all) of an impoverished family: his father was a *tatami* maker. His name at birth was Matsumoto Chizuo: Asahara Shōkō is a name adopted for religious purposes in 1987. He had badly impaired sight, having 30 per cent vision in one eye and being blind in the other, which led him to be sent to study at a special school for the blind, where he boarded for several years. His sight problems did not prevent him from seeking a university education, however: he took, but failed to pass, the university entrance examinations for Kumamoto University. Soon afterwards, in 1977, he moved up to the Tokyo region, where he enrolled in a private school that tutored students to pass university entrance examinations, and he attempted this time to get into Tokyo University. He again failed at the entrance examination stage.

11. See Kitabake 1995: 378–379 as an example of such pop psychologising.
12. I am in complete agreement with Richard Young (1995: 243) when he notes the need for the sort of in-depth analysis of Asahara's personality as was done by James Gordon (1987) on Bhagwan Rajneesh.

However, in 1978 he got married to a woman he had met while studying in Tokyo; his wife, Matsumoto Tomoko (she has retained his original family name) who was then 19, shortly afterwards gave birth to their first child. In all they now have six children, the last being born in 1994, with their third daughter being recognised in Aum as his spiritual heir.[13] His wife Tomoko also became a leading member and practitioner in Aum, able to carry out some of Aum's initiation rituals and becoming a 'minister' in the alternative government Aum established in 1994 (see Chapter 4, below).

During his early years in Tokyo Asahara developed an interest in spiritual matters: he practised acupuncture, sold herbal medicines, and acquired an interest in divination. He also read books on religion and became interested in the teachings of some of the 'new' new religions and their founders. For example, he read works by Takahashi Shinji, the founder of GLA, whose teachings about the multiple levels of the spiritual world and of the different realms to which spirits could ascend or descend at death, and of the predominantly sinful nature of this world, bore some resemblance to Buddhist teachings.[14] He also took an interest in the teachings of Kiriyama Seiyū and the religion he had founded, Agonshū. Kiriyama emphasised in his writings that he had attained various special powers through his practice of austerities, yoga and meditation. He had written a number of volumes proclaiming that those who followed his teachings could have access to special powers normally associated with esoteric Buddhism: in particular he stated that various forms of superhuman powers (*chōnōryoku*) could thus be acquired and that through the esoteric spiritual practices of Agonshū one

---

13. This is rather typical in Japanese religious terms: the charisma of leaders is often considered to be passed on through the blood, and it is the normal case that the founder of a religious movement is succeeded by a direct descendant.

14. Takahashi Shinji (1928– 1976) was an extremely charismatic teacher who claimed to have direct access to various spiritual teachers, including Christ and the Buddha. On Takahashi and GLA see Numata 1987 and 1988. GLA's teachings, and the figure of Takahashi, have also had a profound effect on the development of another 'new' new religion, Kōfuku no Kagaku (see Astley 1995: 346).

could acquire powers to divine the future and to determine one's own fate. [15]

Asahara became a member of Agonshū in 1981 and took part in some of its practices, such as yoga and the *senza gyō*, an Agonshū practice (now no longer used) that demanded a sustained level of commitment from the practitioner, for it involved the chanting of sutras and the performance of acts of worship for approximately 40 minutes a day, on a daily basis for 1000 days. Although he completed this thousand-day practice, Asahara reported that it had been very painful and difficult for him. During this time, too, he suffered a crisis when he was arrested, and subsequently fined, for selling unlicensed herbal medicines, a crisis which affected his wife very badly and led her close to a breakdown.[16] Asahara's arrest and conviction provides an interesting parallel to the life of Agonshū's founder, for Kiriyama Seiyū had himself been arrested and imprisoned in 1953 for vending illegally made alcoholic beverages. This was before he became interested in a religious path, and Kiriyama has subsequently pointed to this incident both as evidence of his previous spiritual weakness which he later overcame through spiritual practice and as a stimulus to him to give up his bad ways and pursue a better life through religious practice.[17]

Such crises are not uncommon in the lives of the founders of new religions in Japan and often provide the stimulus for increased religious practice and effort. In Asahara's case it appears that by 1984 he had become convinced enough of his own spiritual progress to feel capable of leaving Agonshū and establishing a religious movement of his own, the Aum Shinsennokai,[18] which was primarily focused on yoga and had 15 members at the beginning who followed him as their teacher.

---

15. On Agonshū in general see Reader 1988 and 1991 (208–233). Kiriyama, like most leaders of religious movements in Japan, has published prodigiously: the theme of the acquisition of superhuman power is found in much of his work, most notably his first book which became widely known in Japan, *Henshin no Genri* (a title that could be translated as 'the principles of transforming the body') (Kiriyama 1971). Asahara left Agonshū in 1984 and since then has had no connection with them. Agonshū has, understandably, in the light of the Aum affair, been keen to distance itself as much as possible from Asahara and has been extremely reluctant to talk about his earlier involvement with them.

16. Shimazono 1995: 8, Fujita 1995: 82.

17. Reader 1988: 246.

18. The word *shinsen* means hermit, wizard or Taoist sage: hence a literal translation of this title would be 'Aum wizards society'.

Many of the ideas found in Agonshū were transplanted into Aum and became a basis for its subsequent teachings. Besides the interest in superhuman powers acquired through yoga and meditation, Asahara also imbibed Agonshū's millennialism. Arguing that the world has entered a period of crisis at the end of this century due to the accumulated karma[19] of the past, Kiriyama had often predicted the coming of doom in 1999 unless immediate spiritual action were taken to avert it. This focus on cataclysm and on the year 1999 was in part drawn from the prophecies of Nostradamus, which Kiriyama had read with interest, frequently wondering whether he was the saviour from the East mentioned in Nostradamus' writings. Agonshū's millennialism was, however, optimistic in tone, for Kiriyama stated that the disasters threatening the world would be overcome through spiritual action, and that Agonshū had a mission to restore 'true Buddhism' to the world and to spread peace across the globe.[20]

Agonshū had also developed a flair for dramatic presentations of its messages, whether in its huge and highly publicised fire rituals, or through its use of modern technologies, from videos to *manga* (cartoons) and telecommunication satellites, with which it disseminated its word across Japan. While it also saw modern society as a spiritual wasteland, it had no problems with utilising its technologies. Agonshū's skilful use of such means of dissemination brought it immense publicity and rapidly, in the earlier part of the 1980s, turned it from being a small and relatively unknown movement, to being well known throughout Japan, with a resultant expansion in its membership.

This clearly provided a model for Asahara, for throughout subsequent Aum history we see a continual drive to achieve maximum publicity for his teachings, both through the use of *manga* and videos and through public displays of the prowess that Asahara and Aum members claimed to have achieved through their ascetic practices. Asahara publicised the movement by proclaiming that he had acquired extraordinary powers through his yogic practices, and photographs of him levitating (or, rather, leaping in full lotus position in the air in a manner reminiscent of the disciples of Transcendental Meditation) appeared in the esoteric magazine *Twilight Zone* in February 1985. The promise of

---

19. The term karma (Japanese: *karuma*) invariably has a negative connotation when used by Japanese new religions such as Agonshū.
20. Reader 1991: 212–215.

acquiring such powers served as a magnet attracting followers, and in the next few years Aum began to gradually grow in the Tokyo region.

In the period leading up to 1986 he had a number of religious experiences which intensified his sense of spiritual power, culminating in a visit to the Himalayas in 1986 when he claimed to have attained absolute enlightenment: on his return he declared himself to be the single, most exalted and spiritually advanced being in Japan. He also began to publish books on the acquisition of superhuman spiritual powers[21] and to preach to his followers that they could develop these through following him. In 1987 he assumed the name Asahara Shōkō[22] and changed the group's name to Aum Shinrikyō, the name under which it was eventually registered, in August 1989, under the Religious Corporations Law.

World Rejection and Millennialism

Aum's theology from early on was, as we have seen, underpinned by the notion that the world was predominantly sinful, and that life was primarily a process of suffering. Such ideas emphasised the importance of escaping from suffering through spiritual practice, and of finding reality not in the world of substance but in spiritual disciplines such as meditation. Thus Aum, in contrast to the positivistic attitudes of most Japanese new religions, which offer their followers the potential for realisation, success and achievement in this world, not only asserted a critical and antithetical view of society and of Japanese materialism, but asserted the importance of withdrawing from it to practice austerities. This apparently idealistic rejection of wealth and materialism in favour of spiritual progress through asceticism, yoga and meditation attracted to it young, idealistic people who were dissatisfied or disillusioned by the materialism, stifling conformity, rigid structures and competitiveness of Japanese society.

Aum's world-rejectionism was closely linked to its millennialism which promised the conquest of the corrupt material

---

21. See, for example, Asahara 1986. The title of this book *Chōnōryoku: himitsu no kaihatsuhō* translates roughly as 'Superhuman power: the secret means of development'.

22. Changing one's name for religious purposes is not uncommon in Japan; for example Buddhist priests usually take a new name upon ordination, as do some new religious leaders.

world and the triumph of a new, spiritually aware, civilisation. Aum felt the world was consumed by materialism, ravaged by environmental disasters and threatened by mass warfare as a result of the collapse of political and moral authority. Like Agonshū, though, it also initially believed the world could be saved and transformed through spiritual action. Aum's vision until the late 1980s stated that the coming crisis, which was caused by a build-up of negative spiritual energy in the world, could be averted through the emergence of 30,000 renunciates (Japanese: *shukkesha*) or spiritually enlightened people, whose positive energies would eradicate the negative and help create an ideal world.[23] It was, of course, through Asahara's leadership and Aum's activities that these enlightened renunciates would be produced. However, since the cataclysm that these renunciates were going to prevent was due to happen, according to Aum, in 1999, it meant that the movement had comparatively little time in which to persuade 30,000 people to turn their backs on the world and become *shukkesha*.

As is common in millennial movements, the vision of what the world would look like when the millennium was realised was vague, although in Aum's vision it involved the advent of a messiah (Asahara, who came to see himself as a Christ figure) and the establishment of a utopian society in which people would live for an immensely long time. It also clearly involved the notion of a union between religion and politics, for Aum talked of building Shambala (the ideal Buddhist kingdom united under religious law) on earth. In preparation for this it embarked, in 1988, on a project to build self-sufficient communal villages known as Lotus Villages throughout Japan, where its members could live together and develop their spiritual consciousness away from the temptations and negativity of the everyday world. Japan was thus to be the land where Aum would construct a utopian society: this plan, however, along with the drive to create a large group of renunciates, was a factor leading Aum into disputes and confrontations with the outside world.

---

23. Mainichi Shinbun Shūkyō Shuzaihan (ed.) 1993: 131 cites this as a basic Aum belief: it has been widely cited elsewhere, e.g. in the entry on Aum in the 1991 *Shinshūkyō jiten* (the major dictionary on new religions in Japan), and by Hardacre 1995: 16. However, I have yet to see any citations as to where it has been mentioned in Aum literature, and the figure is not found in any Aum publications I have seen from later than the 1989–1990 period.

Renunciation, Asceticism and the Demonstration of Power

Those who joined Aum were encouraged to give up their worldly status and become *shukkesha* (renunciates). The term *shukke* means to leave home, and is the traditional word describing what Buddhist monks do, i.e. renounce their families and worldly possessions for a monastic existence of poverty. This concept of renunciation was a radical departure from the normal patterns not only of the new religions but also of Buddhism in the present day, for Japanese Buddhist priests normally now marry, take over their fathers' temples and own property. It also conflicted with prevailing Japanese social mores, which place great emphasis on family solidarity and on the obedience of the young towards their parents. It was as a result of young people apparently spurning their families to go and live in Aum communes and cutting off all contact with their families, that increasing numbers of complaints were made by troubled families against Aum, and this led to the emergence of stories in the media accusing Aum of being a religion whose perspective was antithetical to the social ethos of Japanese society.

Those who became *shukkesha* were required to leave their families, cutting off all contacts with them, and signing over all their property and wealth to Aum. They pledged devotion to their guru (Asahara) who set out the path they should tread to enlightenment, and who both encouraged and verified their progress along the way. Renunciates undertook a severe path of austerity, fasting, meditating, yogic practices, and living in communal rural settings. Ascetic practice and renunciation were believed to lead to the attainment of numerous powers, ranging from the ability to levitate and to be clairvoyant, to the power to travel through the various spiritual realms. Asahara's teaching proclaimed that there is a hierarchy of spiritual realms through which spirits transmigrate, with those who have lived bad lives being consigned, at death, to an existence in the lower realms and those who live spiritually beneficial lives being reincarnated in higher realms. According to Aum, Asahara, the guru, was also able to intercede at death to protect his followers and guide them to higher realms, and as has been mentioned, to conduct rituals to enable the spirits of the dead to reach higher levels in the spirit world.[24]

---

24. For an outline of these ideas and points see Aum Translation Committee (ed) 1992.

The spiritual disciplines that the renunciates followed were, at least in some respects, not all that dissimilar to traditional Zen Buddhist monastic disciplines in Japan: meditation, early rising, physical work, spartan vegetarian food, chanting, having no possessions beyond those needed for basic living, and a small (one *tatami* mat) space to sleep on. To some people this focus on asceticism was what made Aum appear attractive: as Richard Young has noted, 'ascetic practice was a symptomatically attractive feature of AUM' and that (in his initial impressions based on a visit to an Aum centre):

> there might even be a certain value in its enforcement of a tough Buddhist regimen, unlike the coddling, feel-good-about-the-ancestors-but-to-hell-with-the-precepts attitude of established Buddhism.[25]

Asahara was convinced of the value of ascetic practice and believed that it led to extraordinary physical powers that could be used to demonstrate 'scientifically' the validity of his teachings. Just as earlier proclamations of his ability to levitate had been used to demonstrate both his own spiritual prowess and the efficacy of his teachings, so too did Aum make use of subsequent physical achievements that came as a result of its ascetic practices.

Thus, in the latter 1980s Aum members, including Asahara, claimed, amongst other things, the ability to suspend virtually all bodily functions such as breathing for long periods, through their mastery of yoga techniques. Demonstrations were put on for the media to draw attention to such achievements: in October 1989, for instance, an Aum practitioner performed what Aum termed 'underwater *samadhi*' by remaining fully submerged underwater (in public view and under the eyes of the media) for almost 15 minutes – a proof, according to Aum, of his attained spiritual release. Other such feats included Asahara and a leading female disciple, Ishii Hisako (whose Indian initiatory name was Kheema Taishi) being immersed for 12 hours in an airtight box underwater (with in theory only enough air to last them for half that time) and various underground 'burials' of practitioners in airtight containers for several days at a time. In each case the tests were verified by the media and scientific experts, and announcements of these feats were accompanied in Aum publications by charts

25. Young 1995: 238.

depicting how the practitioners had managed to control their blood, heart and breathing rates to almost nothing.[26]

Such demonstrations were, in Aum's eyes, proof of its ability to produce a community of advanced beings who had transcended the boundaries of normal human ability and who would, thus, be capable of surviving the cataclysm that was predicted. It is clear also that Asahara placed great faith in the importance of such tests, for they appeared to demonstrate scientifically that his methods worked. The ability of his followers to go without oxygen and emerge unharmed – and to be able to demonstrate by the use of medical charts and graphs that they had been able to exert such control on their physical bodies – thus was seen as 'proving' the truth of Aum's claims. Although science, in the form of scientific rationalism and materialism, could be seen as dangerous and as leading humanity towards danger and destruction, it could also be called upon to validate the truths preached by Aum.

Such a path of severe ascetic discipline struck a deep chord for some followers, who plunged into increasingly strict training in the search of ever higher levels of achievement. Many appeared to have benefitted from it: as Fujita Shōichi has shown, through his interviews with a number of Aum's ascetic practitioners, including Asahara's wife Tomoko, in 1991, the renunciates considered that they had achieved quite striking effects as a result of their practices, and that their lives had been transformed as a result. It is also chilling to note, as Fujita does, that many of those happy renunciates he interviewed then have since been arrested and charged with crimes of violence.[27]

Asceticism, Coercion and the Seeds of Failure

The forms of asceticism practised in Aum became more strict the longer the movement carried on, and there appears to have been an increasing insistence on asceticism as *the* means of liberation. Asahara developed not just an extreme faith in its value but a growing conviction that people had to be *made* to do ascetic practices if they were to attain liberation or to avoid destruction in the Armageddon which he began to see more and more as a certainty. Thus ascetic practice was not only encouraged but even

---

26. See, for example, Asahara 1991: 30–40, and Asahara (ed.) 1992: 32.
27. See Fujita 1995: 103–134 for these interviews and comments.

enforced. People were coerced and intimidated into doing austerities: his wife, for example, had displayed no inclination to perform austerities until 1988 when Asahara, apparently convinced that it was necessary for her well-being, forced her against her will to do so, a point she herself affirmed in an interview with Fujita Shōichi in 1991.[28]

The enforcement of harsh physical disciplines at times seems to have led to a blurring of the lines between encouragement, coercion and violence, and appears, from recent reports, to have occasioned the first acts of violence inside the movement. It is perhaps also worth noting that no one in the movement had any serious training in austerities and ascetic traditions, and that this might have been a factor in its inability to protect its members thoroughly in their practice, or to stop enforcing such practices when they were causing damage to members.[29] At any rate, something appears to have gone wrong in this respect sometime toward the end of 1988 or the beginning of 1989, when a follower died accidentally while doing austerities at an Aum centre. This in turn led one of those involved in the death, Taguchi Shūji, who was 25 years old at the time and who had become a *shukkesha* in 1988, to develop doubts and fears about Aum's teachings. He decided to leave the movement but apparently was killed before he could do so.[30]

Asceticism thus, whilst pointing towards attainment and the acquisition of the hoped-for superhuman powers and to the validation of Aum's teaching, also produced its negative effects,

---

28. Fujita 1995: 120–121.

29. Steinhoff 1992: 200, makes the point, in explaining how things went wrong in the Rengō Sekigun, that the group established consciousness-raising therapies that none of those present really knew how to control, since they had no training in the matter. Hence they were incapable of stopping the process when it became dangerous to participants. I think one could make a similar point about Aum: despite Asahara's studies of yoga, etc, he had not formally trained in a discipline or tradition, and hence neither he nor his followers had any training in controlling the potential excesses of their practices or in understanding when these might become harmful to their members.

30. At present I have no further details about this case: the above details are taken from a report in the *Japan Times* of Nov. 12 1995, and I am grateful for Robert Kisala for sending this information to me. This piece of news has come out very recently and at this point I do not know who is alleged to have carried out the killing, and why Aum leaders felt it was necessary to kill Taguchi rather than let him leave. It is especially unfortunate that more information is at this point not available on the Taguchi case as it appears, as far as we currently know, to be the first killing carried out by Aum.

with the recourse to coercion and violence, which resulted in Aum members being pressurised into asceticism, and which led also to the death of Taguchi and perhaps others. It also produced a number of stark and negative images connected with the group when, as mentioned in the Introduction, televison viewers were shown the sight of emaciated Aum renunciates in states of near collapse due to the sparse nature of their diets and the extremities of their practice, being carried away from Kamikuishiki in ambulances after the raids of March 22 1995.

The severity of Aum's asceticism and the extreme demands of renunciation also proved a serious impediment to the growth in the numbers of *shukkesha*.[31] In all around 1,200 members eventually became *shukkesha*, although until 1993 this number was far lower. Between 1986 and 1990, 537 people took this step, with the number growing each year to a peak of 246 in 1990. In 1991 and 1992 (a period when Aum really began to run into trouble with the outside world) the number fell sharply and only 43 people became renunciates in these two years. In the 18 months from January 1993 until summer 1994, however, the numbers swelled, and 524 members became renunciates in this period.[32] This latter growth, however, came at a time when Asahara's prophecies of the coming Armageddon had begun to escalate, and when he had begun to teach that the only way of surviving this final war was by becoming an Aum renunciate.

The slow growth in the number of renunciates is quite crucial, especially if we bear in mind that Aum had a target of 30,000 renunciates before 1999 so that it could save the world. By the end of 1990 it had managed to produce less than 2 per cent of that number and it was running out of time. It is perhaps not surprising, in such terms, that the goals Asahara had earlier stipulated, of saving the whole of humanity, came to be scaled down, and that he began to talk, from around 1989 onwards, of

---

31. As an example of how the need to renounce one's worldly goods stopped some Aum devotees from taking this step see Mainichi Shinbun Shūkyō Shuzaihan (ed.) 1993: 130–131. This study of Aum Shinrikyō was carried out before the development of major internal tensions at Kamikuishiki, and it cites an interview with a 42-year-old Aum member, staying at the commune with his family and children, who states that although he is a devotee he would not become a renunciate because it would cost too much, in giving up all his family's worldly belongings.

32. See Shimazono 1995: 6, for these figures, which are taken from the *Mainichi Shinbun* May 1st 1995.

the possibilities of saving only a section of it. The demands made
of those who became renunciates worked to prevent all but a few
taking this path: hence the deep faith placed in austerities as a
means of salvation and as a proof of the movement's efficacy, was
also a barrier against the expansion that Aum needed if it were to
fulfil its mission.

Guru, Initiation and the Hierarchy of Attainment

Asahara was both the source of religious inspiration and the
focus of devotion in Aum. It was his achievements (supreme
enlightenment, leading to his becoming, in Aum's view, the most
spiritually advanced being in Japan) that placed him in this
position, and enabled him to supervise the strivings of his
followers. It was he who bestowed recognition of spiritual
attainment on his disciples, and he who transferred, through
initiation rituals, his own powers to others. Aum developed the
view that there was a hierarchic path to liberation via a series of
stages marked out by a structured series of initiations, each of
which represented a further step upwards.[33] One of the first and
most common initiations in Aum was the *shaktipat* initiation. In
this initiation, which is derived from Hinduism, the guru
(Asahara) absorbed the disciple's negative karma by placing his
thumb on the disciple's forehead where the third eye is believed
to be located. Eventually Asahara ceased to perform this
initiation because, it was claimed, the transference of negative
karma into his body denuded him of strength and made him ill:
subsequently other leading followers, including his wife,
Tomoko, took over performing this initiation. Although leading
disciples were thus considered capable of high levels of
attainment, and indeed gave lectures and played a major role in
spreading Aum's teachings, Asahara remained the source of final
power, granting members promotion through Aum's spiritual
ranks, and remaining the only person who had attained the
highest states of spiritual achievement.

Asahara's status was affirmed by his numerous claims and
assertions of spiritual rank. As we have seen, he was the saviour
predicted by Nostradamus, the Christ come to establish the new

---

33. See Aum Shinrikyō (ed.), n.d. *Shugyo* pp. 10–11 for a detailed outline of
the various levels and types of initiation that were available to Aum
members in the 1990s.

spiritual kingdom, and the supremely enlightened one who would build the new spiritual kingdom after the millennium. Such assumptions of grandeur were reflected in an increasingly impressive array of titles by which Aum referred to him. He was described as 'the spirit of supreme truth: the most holy, Master Asahara Shōkō' (*shinri no mitama: saishō Asahara Shōkō sonshi*) and was titled (in Aum's alternative, or parallel, government which was formed in 1994) 'Sacred/divine emperor or king' (*shinsei hōō*),[34] a title that reflects Aum's and Asahara's increasingly theocratic tendencies.

While extreme devotion to the leader is a common feature of Japanese new religions, many of which regard their founders and leaders not just as sources of power and charismatic authority, but also as living deities (*ikigami*), few religions have extended this as far as did Aum. It established a series of initiatory rituals in which Asahara's powers were transferred to his followers, thus enabling them to rise higher in the spiritual world. In so doing, the initiations served to enhance Asahara's own status and power further, for they emphasised the physical powers inherent in his own body, and the traces of Asahara's physical body in themselves became sources of spiritual energy to be used in various initiations. Strands of his hair could be carried on one's person as a spiritual defence against dangers, or if infused in hot water, that water would be transformed into spiritually energising nectar.[35]

Eventually a whole series of initiatory rituals involving Asahara's physical traces developed, each costing his disciples increasing amounts of money. Thus his bath water could be drunk to imbibe his spiritual energy, and his blood be imbibed to absorb his DNA through which his spiritual forces were taken into his disciples bodies.[36] Ultimately, too, such practices designed to draw the disciple closer to the master included the wearing of PSI (Perfect Salvation Initiation) units mentioned in the Introduction, which were rented for a month at a time.

---

34. The term *hōō* signifies the (Buddhist) notion of the dharma king, or king of the (Buddhist) law, a ruler who is both a political and a spiritual leader.

35. Aum Shinrikyō (ed.), n.d. *Shugyō* p. 23.

36. There have been allegations that people undergoing such initiations were actually fed hallucinogenic drugs in the water or blood they imbibed. Certainly there are several accounts of followers who underwent such initiations reporting extraordinary sensations as a result, which at the time they attributed to Asahara's powers (for fuller details see Fujita 1995: 39–41).

Initiation and the Costs of Enlightenment

All these initiations, besides intensifying the followers' dependence on the leader as source of charisma and power and emphasising the idea that they always had another stage, another level of attainment to reach in order to get close to his levels of power and achievement, also cost increasing amounts of money (300,000 yen, or over US$ 3,000 for a phial of blood, one million yen to rent the PSI headgear for a month). Such initiations were one means by which Aum raised money: others included the various membership and meditation fees paid by ordinary members and the donation by renunciates of all their worldly goods and savings, and at times of those of their families as well. Aum eventually also developed various business ventures such as computer shops and noodle bars to generate further resources.[37] The monies raised were used to purchase land for its communes, which became increasingly necessary to Aum as a setting where it could train its ascetics, and to finance its publications and efforts to attract new members. Eventually, such monies were also used to finance the building of the laboratories and the purchase of raw materials which were used to create weapons of destruction, as well as to stockpile resources for the coming of Armageddon.

Some of Aum's problems can be traced to the financial demands it placed upon itself in order to carry out its plans to build communes and prepare for the new world. To maintain renunciates who, once they had joined, could provide no further direct income, was itself costly, while the drive to build communes and to acquire land placed large financial burdens on the movement. Such concerns, I consider, played a major role in what, especially from around 1993 onwards, became an extraordinarily aggressive pattern of seeking money not just from its followers but also from their family members. There appears to have been an escalating cycle in which resources were acquired in order to finance building and proselytisation schemes, and – as

---

37. Aum's activities in running various restaurants produced, for me, one of the few amusing elements in the whole affair: in the media stampede to run stories demonising Aum, one weekly, amidst a tirade of 'Aum victim stories', recounted the experiences of a woman who had gone to eat in an Aum noodle shop, and who thought the food was terrible (*Aera* No. 23, 5/25, 1995, p. 22). Not only was Aum guilty of mass murder, extortion and kidnapping, it seems, but it even sinned against the Japanese love of (and obsession with) good food!

the Aum view of Armageddon drew closer – to finance its preparations for that event. These activities have subsequently resulted in various criminal charges of extortion being levelled against several senior Aum figures.

In terms of Aum's view of the material world as corrupt, it might appear ironic that it placed such a high price on, and indeed appears to have sold, the symbols and rituals of the attainment of spiritual status. It should also be noted, however, that for those who believed they were about to see the collapse of the material civilisation of the present, and their emergence into an idealised post-millennium world where they would have superhuman powers and transcendent knowledge and happiness, the forfeiting of mere worldly goods now (to be used to build for their future and to prepare for the coming of the millennium) might appear small sacrifices. Those who joined Aum and were convinced enough by its teachings and Asahara's charisma to renounce the world were entering into what one might term the 'enlightenment contract' or the 'salvation contract' in which a product, in this case an ideal(ised) or imagined state of being, is offered in return for sacrifices. Whilst this may not justify the demands made by Aum on its members, or its apparent exploitation of them, it does at least go some way towards showing why some members were ready to accept these demands, at least initially. The story of one Aum renunciate called Masao, which was discussed in a volume on the new religions produced by the Mainichi newspaper group, exemplifies these points, and also suggests why, for some Aum seemed attractive enough to donate large sums of money to. Masao was aged 32: he had grown up outside Tokyo but had gone there at the age of 18 to make a living. He worked delivering newspapers but found this unsatisfactory and quit. He then studied acupuncture and became interested in various religions, including Agonshū, before joining Aum. He sensed a reality in the spiritual world he met through Aum that he had not found in society, and came to feel he was a disciple of Buddha: thus he resolved to renounce the world and was in training to become a *shukkesha*.

In so doing he had expended considerable amounts of money: a 300,000 yen donation to study meditation, 100,000 yen for a cup of water with a drop of Asahara's DNA in it, and so on until, at the time of becoming a renunciate, he had given over 5 million yen to the movement. He had trained for one year as a renunciate before starting to have doubts, eventually deciding to leave the movement and returning to lay life. Even though he had done so he apparently did not resent the relationship with Aum for he continued to yearn for the acquisition of the superhuman powers he had sought in Aum, and continued to receive and read its magazine every month. Clearly, too, during the whole process of donating money to Aum and paying for increasing levels of practice and initiation he had felt that he was attaining something on which a monetary value could not be placed, and even after giving up the life of a *shukkesha* he continued to be interested in Aum and to speak warmly about it.[38]

Conclusions to Chapter One

Formed in the mid-1980s with idealistic intentions of world salvation and of developing a strict order of renunciates, Aum was by 1989 a small millennialist movement perhaps best known to the general public (if known at all) because of its public demonstrations of ascetic activities, and because of the striking clothes and appearance of its leader. At this stage, Aum appeared on the surface to be just another of the many new religions active in late-twentieth-century Japan, albeit one with a countenance and perspectives that were rather different from most of the others. However, there were already some signs of tension and violence beneath the surface in the increasing pressures placed upon members to perform austerities and in the extreme forms such austerities took. Also, as the slow growth in the numbers of *shukkesha* showed, Aum was beginning to encounter difficulties in its self-proclaimed mission to the world. In 1989 and 1990, however, these problems escalated dramatically, when Aum achieved national prominence, notoriety and public rejection in a way that intensified its world-rejectionism. It is to this sequence of events that I shall turn in the next chapter.

---

38. Mainichi Shinbun Shūkyō Shuzaihan (ed.) 1993: 127–130.

Chapter 2

Aum against the World
Conflict, Rejection and Reaction

The Growth of External Conflicts: the Application for Legal Religious Status

In Chapter 1 we saw that internal coercion had begun to appear in Aum by 1988, when Matsumoto Tomoko, Asahara's wife, was made to undertake austerities. Voices had come to be raised against the movement by early 1989 by the parents of some of those who had gone off to become Aum *shukkesha*. This became clear in April 1989 when Aum filed an application in the Tokyo prefectural government offices for registration under the Religious Corporations Law (*shūkyō hōjin hō*). Such a step is a fairly normal one in the development of a religious movement in Japan, for registration confers a number of benefits, including tax privileges, the right to own property as an organisation, and protection from any state or other external interference. Although there are over 180,000 organisations registered under this act, the vast majority of them are individual Shinto shrines or Buddhist temples which have registered as religious organisations for tax reasons. The actual number of separate religious movements is far less, however, probably several hundred in all, including new religions, established Buddhist sects and Shinto organisations, as well as Christian groups.[1] Aum filed its application in Tokyo, where

---

1.   It is important to stress that the number of religious movements in Japan, whilst quite large, is not as extensive as portrayed by the media and, indeed, some academics in the immediate aftermath of the Aum affair. Although there are over 180,000 institutions registered under *shūkyō hōjin* laws, this does not mean there are that many religious movements in Japan: a more reasonable estimate would be less than one per cent of this figure!

its main activities at the time were based. Such applications are normally investigated by the regional office where they are made and, if successful, the religious body concerned is registered throughout Japan.

Although, given the numbers of individual religious institutions registered under this law, Aum must have felt its application would be accepted, it in fact ran into trouble and was initially turned down. The Tokyo office had received a number of complaints that Aum was causing splits in families, a complaint based in the practice of *shukkesha* to sever all ties with their families and cease communicating with them. Although the number of *shukkesha* was small, those who did renounce the world were mostly young (their average age in 1994 was 27) and some were under the age of adulthood (20 in Japan). Others, although legally adults, had shocked their parents by giving up promising careers to become *shukkesha*, a shock often intensified when the parents attempted to make contact with their offspring and found that they refused to see them. In some cases access was directly denied by Aum officials, and this provoked complaints (at this stage almost certainly incorrect) that Aum as an organisation was denying its members access to their families and was effectively seeking to split families up.[2]

Aum's response to this setback was to go on the offensive. Asahara and his followers protested loudly and publicly about the rejection of their application, mounting demonstrations around the prefectural office, issuing law suits and making a legal appeal against the decision. These protests brought Aum into some public prominence: it became a news item for a while and the publicity made the movement quite widely known in Japan.

---

2. The charge that new religions 'break families up' is frequently made in the media in general and by the families of those who have become followers of movements deemed not to fit in with mainstream society (such charges have frequently, for example, been levelled against the Unification Church). However, there is little serious academic evidence to substantiate such claims (see Barker 1984), and in the Aum Shinrikyō case in the late 1980s the evidence is that those who became *shukkesha* simply did not want to return to their old lifestyles in the ordinary world and that they were so driven by the desire for enlightenment or liberation that they were prepared to cut off ties with their families: Mainichi Shinbun Shūkyō Shuzaihan (ed) 1993: 133 cites a young *shukkesha* who in 1990 bluntly stated (in a television interview on this issue) that he did not want to return to his parents. Later, however, he decided to leave Aum and (at least in 1993) was living with his mother (ibid. p. 134).

The protests were successful, and Aum was granted legal status as a religious organisation in August 1989.[3]

It is difficult to know exactly what the effect of this initial rejection and the ways Aum dealt with it had on Aum's subsequent thinking, but one can perhaps suggest that it read two things into the events. The first was that the outside world, the world of the mainstream materialist society which Aum saw as heading for disaster unless it became more spiritually conscious, was inimical towards the movement. This was a feeling that gradually grew, as Aum became involved in increasing numbers of conflicts, into feelings of persecution which developed in the period from 1993 onwards into a series of allegations of conspiracies against Aum. The second was that its aggressive response to the rejection had borne fruit, not just in getting the application for religious status accepted but in gaining publicity and attention for the movement. The affair thus set something of a pattern for Aum's behaviour whenever it ran into difficulties and faced allegations or investigations in the future: subsequently it responded to every allegation or hint of misdeed with vigorous denials, law suits and the like. It thus used apparent adversities to gain further attention and publicise itself, whilst also, perhaps, gaining the impression that it could overcome any external problem through aggressive responses. As such, adversity became deeply woven into the fabric of Aum's thinking, playing a growing role in Aum's understanding of itself and of the ways it saw itself vis-a-vis the outside world, and serving as an opportunity for increasing its profile in the world.

Media Exposés and the Sakamoto Affair

The complaints against Aum, however, led to a series of investigations into the movement by newspapers and by a lawyer from Yokohama, named Sakamoto Tsutsumi, who had been contacted by some concerned parents of Aum members in May 1989. Sakamoto had had previous experience of dealing with conflicts between parents and offspring who joined

3. This status has come under review since March 1995, although any consideration of Aum's registration under this law has been superceded by the judgement banning Aum under the Subversive Activities Prevention Law.

religious groups and had been recommended to the parents as such.[4] The *Sunday Mainichi* magazine also began to examine Aum and, in October 1989, began a seven-part series on the movement, accusing it of being a religion that broke up families and that exploited its followers. Amongst its accusations were that those who joined Aum were separated from their families and not allowed any interaction with them, that their children were not given any (formal) schooling, and that members were made to give large donations to the movement: in particular, it focused on the blood initiation as an example of the movement's ways of gaining donations from its followers.

As a result of its articles, the *Sunday Mainichi* received over 200 letters and postcards from people airing grievances against Aum, both from the families of those who had joined and from former members of Aum. The magazine helped these people get in touch with each other and with Sakamoto and, as a result, a pressure group, the *Aum Shinrikyō higaisha no kai* (Aum Shinrikyō Victims' Society) was established, with Sakamoto as its legal representative. Aum responded angrily to the *Sunday Mainichi* exposés, attempting to take the editors and senior executives of the Mainichi news group to court, campaigning vociferously against the magazine and publishing a series of attacks against it.

Sakamoto uncovered evidence that Aum was using false information in its attempts to get members to undergo the blood initiation. Aum had claimed that Asahara's blood had been analysed at the laboratories of Kyoto University and found to contain a special form of DNA unique to him. It was this unique form of DNA that could be imbibed in the blood initiation, thus enhancing the initiate's spiritual powers. Sakamoto was able to acquire clear proof that no such tests had ever been carried out. As a result he became convinced that he was not merely dealing with a case of a conflictual religion whose practices offended against mainstream values, but one which resorted to lies and untruths in

---

4.   This was done by the journalist Egawa Shōko, who knew Sakamoto and had contacts with one of the parents involved. Egawa subsequently began her own investigation of Aum and published a number of critical pieces about Aum and Asahara both before and after the March 1995 raids. These publications led her to face, she has stated, a number of hostile responses from Aum. Egawa has also talked in her frequent television interviews of her sense of responsibility for the fate of the Sakamoto family, since she first brought Sakamoto into the affair (see also Egawa 1995).

order to pursue its goals, and that this was therefore a matter not for the civil courts but the criminal ones. Although he held out hopes of reaching some form of agreement when he met Aum's lawyers, he was disappointed in this and in fact received a hostile response from them. Sakamoto had, according to Egawa, assumed he would be able to deal reasonably with Aum's legal representatives because they would, as lawyers, be of a similar bent to himself. However, he was wrong in this; he reported to Egawa Shōko that Aum's legal representatives were not inclined to deal with him as a fellow lawyer or to discuss the issue dispassionately because they were all followers of Asahara. Aum's legal team was headed by Aoshima Yoshinobu, a young lawyer who eventually became Aum's Minister of Justice in its alternative government, and who was, in 1995, himself arrested on a number of criminal charges.[5]

In early November 1989 Sakamoto disappeared along with his wife and baby son: traces of blood were found in his apartment and an Aum badge was found at the scene. This raised suspicions that the family had been abducted and murdered, and that Aum was somehow involved. The group strongly denied any involvement, asserting that it was being set up by someone, and that the badge had been left to put suspicion on it. Asahara and other Aum spokespeople used the furore caused by the affair to gain publicity and strove to put on a friendly face for the media, granting interviews and appearing on television shows to demonstrate their lack of involvement and to counteract the charges of anti-social attitudes being levelled against them. At the time, investigations did not uncover any direct evidence against the movement, and the fact that the police did not appear to be pursuing the 'Aum connection' in this case appeared to give the movement a clean bill of health.[6]

Admittedly the hint of complicity remained in some quarters: in March 1990, for example, the *Sunday Mainichi*, in a subsequent article about Aum, reported the Sakamoto incident in such a

---

5.   For a general account of these matters see Egawa (1995: 12-18).
6.   Asahara was allowed to travel abroad at this time, and this appeared to suggest that the police were not seriously considering him as a suspect. In December, for example, he went to Germany as part of Aum's overseas efforts, and there he held a press conference denying any involvement in the affair.

manner that the reader could not help drawing links between the disappearances and the religion,[7] and various lawyers groups also publicly demanded that Aum be further investigated on the matter.[8] However, Aum managed to utilise the incident to get publicity and to gain a forum through which to propagate its messages, and it enabled Asahara to appear several times on television, to give interviews and talk about Aum. Photographs of him on television talk shows, discussing Aum's teaching with various famous personalities, subsequently became a common feature and source of legitimation in future Aum publications, thereby further advancing the religion's friendly face towards the public.

In reality, as we now know, the Sakamoto family had been killed by Aum: in June 1995 a group of leading Aum members confessed to the abductions and murders, stating that they were acting on Asahara's orders. The bodies were buried far away from Yokohama: they were discovered in September 1995 as a result of the confessions, and memorial services have since been conducted for the Sakamoto family.[9]

The Sakamoto case was, as far as is known, the first externalised act of violence by Aum, although, as is now known, it had already committed at least one killing inside the movement, of Taguchi earlier in 1989. The killing of Sakamoto, as far as is currently known,[10] was carried out to rid Aum of a thorn in its side that had the potential for causing the movement great harm, at a time when it had begun to feel exposed and to experience external hostility because of the *Sunday Mainichi* series, the formation of the Aum Shinrikyō Victims' Society, and Sakamoto's investigations. Aum leaders had already demonstrated that a fairly thin line existed

---

7. *Sunday Mainichi* 1990, 3/11 pp. 204-207. I came across this article while on a visit to Japan in March 1990. Reading it left me with with no doubt that the magazine wanted the reader to link Aum with the Sakamoto family disappearance.

8. See the chronology given in *Shūkan Yomiuri* 1995, 6/1, pp. 64-65 for the various statements and actions of lawyers' organisations at this time.

9. In an interesting piece of timing, a public memorial service for the family was held in Yokohama in October 1995, only few days before Asahara was originally supposed to have gone on trial charged with various counts of murder and conspiracy to murder.

10. The prosecution case against the six members accused of the murders alleges that they were carried out because of fears that Sakamoto's activities would ruin Asahara's intended bid for political office (see below, p. 43-44) (Asahi News Internet Service, March 12 1996).

within the movement between voluntary action and coercion, and that it was ready to cross this line when it felt necessary. Perhaps also the killing of Taguchi, at the time unknown outside of Aum, was also a factor: the internal pressure created because of his death may have caused Aum's leaders to be doubly sensitive to the investigations of a lawyer such as Sakamoto. Having already once crossed the line and committed murder perhaps also made it easier for Aum leaders to react to external difficulties in a similar vein, in order to remove a troublesome obstacle that it considered was threatening its mission.

Nonetheless, the reaction – killing the Sakamoto family – was out of all proportion to the pressure received. It should be noted that many new religions in Japan have been attacked by the media in similar ways, and that this type of exposé, although unpleasant to the religion concerned, is something that other new religions have also had to endure.[11] Aum in particular should have realised that the type of religion it was (communal, encouraging young people to leave their families behind) and the activities it promoted (getting its members to engage in strict austerities and to pay large sums of money to drink its leader's blood) were bound to attract some negative media attention. Moreover, its flair for the dramatic (which was also attracting media attention at this time because of the demonstrations of power mentioned in Chapter 1) in making unverifiable statements such as those about Asahara's DNA was bound to attract attention. One is led to feel that Aum ought to have realised that such a claim would be examined by someone, given that complaints were being made against it by angry parents of *shukkesha*. This suggests either a remarkable lack of care about what the outside world would do, or an incredible lack of realism. While Aum's leaders seem to have become fearful enough of Sakamoto's investigations – not just the ridicule and exposure they would suffer as a result of his findings over the DNA claim, but also the potential of his continuing opposition to the movement – that they felt they had to kill him, they had also provided him, through their own extravagant claims, with the means and the ammunition with which he could become a serious threat to them.

11. There is a fairly large popular literature of exposés of new religions in Japan, and some sections of the media in particular have a history of such activities. See, e.g., Morioka Kiyomi 1994 on one of the main such events of the 1950s, a campaign by the Yomiuri newspaper group against the new religion Risshō Kōseikai. Such attacks from outside do not necessarily damage new religions; as Morioka shows, the campaign in fact helped strengthen that religion and provided its leadership with a means by which they could reform the movement and increase its size.

Failure and the Growth of Pessimism

During 1989, then, Aum had encountered, and had created for itself, innumerable points of conflict and tension. This was also a period when its failure to grow particularly quickly or to produce as many renunciates as its sense of mission required became evident. Whilst, from an outside perspective, one might not expect a movement of Aum's type, because of its emphasis on communal life and harsh asceticism, to attract vast numbers of followers, Aum leaders can hardly have failed to note that other very new religions were attracting more attention and more members than they were. The 1980s had been a period of major growth for the 'new' new religions. Several had increased their followings dramatically and could claim memberships running into hundreds of thousands: by contrast, Aum had only around 5,000 members at this time, and this must have caused it some misapprehensions, especially when seen in the light of the apparent success of its rivals such as Agonshū and Kōfuku no Kagaku.[12] It had certainly not shown the sort of rapid growth found in many other new religions in their early years, and there are even hints of some stagnation in terms of growth. Perhaps more important, even if the proportion of renunciates (at almost 10

12. Agonshū, for example, increased its following tenfold in the 1980s, while Kōfuku no Kagaku, although still relatively small in 1989, began to grow rapidly in this period and had developed into a large organisation by the early 1990s. The comparison with these two movements is relevant: Agonshū after all was the movement Asahara left in order to form Aum and he doubtless wanted to surpass it, while Kōfuku no Kagaku emerged in Tokyo at roughly the same time as Aum with a leader who made similar claims for himself as the pre-eminent spiritual figure of the age. Both Kōfuku and Aum made similar predictions of catastrophe leading to the millennium, and reinterpreted the writings of Nostradamus to this end. Both appeared to offer their followers the key to attaining transcendent powers and to becoming a member of the chosen elite who would survive the pre-millennial catastrophes to establish, with their leader, the new earthly paradise. The two movements competed to some degree also in their areas of recruitment, each attracting a high proportion of well educated young people from the Tokyo area, and they clashed verbally on many occasions, most famously at an acrimonious television debate in 1991 on Asahi Television. They also traded juvenile insults, each leader analysing the past lives of his rival and coming up with some rather low levels of existence. According to Okawa, Asahara had been Ishikawa Goemon – a notorious brigand of the 17th century who had been executed by being boiled in a cauldron – in his past life, and hence was nothing more than a thief and a murderer, while Asahara announced that Okawa in his previous life had been a *Shikoku no tanuki* (a badger on the island of Shikoku). Kōfuku did not, however, emphasise renunciation and asceticism: nor did it express the sorts of anti-Japanese attitudes that came to the fore in Aum (indeed, Kōfuku has a strongly nationalistic underpinning to it) and attracted many more followers than Aum. Kōfuku claimed to have several million members by 1995 and if this claim is heavily over-inflated (see Shimada 1995: 90–92 and Numata 1995: 193–198), it is nonetheless certain that it was much more successful at getting followers than Aum.

per cent of the total membership) was quite high, Aum had not managed to attract these in the numbers its proclaimed mission of saving the world from disaster required: there were less than 400 *shukkesha*, as we have seen, by the end of 1989, while in 1991 and 1992 the flow of renunciates virtually dried up, only to be increased again by excessive persuasion and coercion.

To what extent an impending sense of failure, or a growing concern that the movement was not meeting its self-imposed goals, created internal tensions and pressures within Aum and was a factor in its actions is at present little more than a matter of conjecture. It is something, however, that needs to be considered as a factor in the confluence of events that drew Aum down the path of violence: as the prospect of the pre-millennial catastrophe came closer, this failure in numerical terms must have had some effects on its thinking, not just in increasing its pessimism about the world at large, but in terms of increasing pressure on itself to find some other way to deal with the crisis.

Certainly by the end of 1989 signs of pessimism had become visible in Asahara's view of the future. His ideas about the nature of the coming of the millennium also began to be coloured by Christian images, which derived in part from his reading of the Book of Revelations, and which brought the concept of Armageddon to the fore of Aum thought.[13] The concept of saving all of humanity disappeared around this time: in his 1989 book *Metsubō no hi* (which bore the stark English sub-title Doomsday - a term which later became affixed to Aum by the media after March 1995 when it became labelled the 'Doomsday cult' in the press) Asahara's predictions of wars and the collapse of civilisations heralded an increasingly pessimistic view of what Aum could achieve in terms of salvation. Earlier optimistic ideas of preventing catastrophe disappeared and Armageddon's destructive inevitability became a reality. All Aum could do would be to limit its damage.

Into the 1990s: Failure, Humiliation and Retreat

Just before the Sakamoto killings, in July 1989, Asahara made a decision that reflected both Aum's penchant for sensation and drama and its thorough misreading of the realities of the world. He told his followers that spiritual action alone was not sufficient to

13. According to Shimazono (1995: 31) he read and began to discuss Revelations in 1988.

change the world and avert the cataclysm, and that therefore Aum needed to take political action. It would establish a political profile by forming a political party, the *Shinritō* (Supreme Truth party) to campaign in the February 1990 Upper House elections.[14] Its aim was to publicise Aum's teachings, to offer everyone salvation from the cataclysm that Asahara was increasingly talking about in his sermons, and to provide Aum with a political base which could be used to this end. The result, however, was a disaster: the party put up 25 candidates, including Asahara, all of whom lost very badly. It appears that they had expected to do well, and Asahara had predicted that he would come top of the ballot. Instead, he was heavily defeated, receiving only 1783 votes in all (in fact he was not even the leading Aum candidate, for Jōyu Fumihiro got more votes than him). The election caused further legal problems, with a lawyers' group which was still pursuing Aum because of the Sakamoto disappearance, issuing writs against Aum charging that it had committed violations of electoral laws and accusing it of having fraudulently changed the residential registrations of several hundred Aum members so they could be voters in Asahara's constituency.

The Aum campaign itself was widely ridiculed, for it consisted largely of members donning Asahara masks and elephant masks signifying the Hindu deity Ganesh, and putting on song and dance performances and singing a ditty that endlessly repeated his name as they tried to attract people on the Tokyo streets. Although some members of the public found the spectacle rather amusing, if a trifle annoying,[15] the campaign attracted immense scorn from the media. Some people felt that the levels of derision were excessive, as these words by Richard Young indicate, when he speaks of:

> the AUM-bashing that became almost a national pastime and a media-obsession in the aftermath of the Master's predictably abject

---

14. The reasons for this seemingly extraordinary decision are unclear, although there has been some speculation that the decision was connected to Aum's problems in acquiring recognition under the Religious Corporations Law, and that Aum felt this problem was in part caused by opposition to it from local politicians. Thus it decided it needed to establish its own political clout to counteract such opposition.

15. The repetitiveness of the song certainly got on the nerves of several people I talked to in Tokyo: one colleague even mentioned that he found himself inadvertently singing the repetitive refrain 'Shōkō, Shōkō' from the Aum campaign song, so often had he heard it!

defeat ... They lost: but why did their noses have to be rubbed in the dirt?[16]

The humiliations resulting from this public rejection intensified Aum's own gradual estrangement from the world: one is tempted to speculate that this rejection, when in Aum's eyes Japanese society spurned the chance to be saved (or perhaps, in Aum's view, was too stupid, too mired in the swamp of contemporary decadence to be saved), might well have pushed Aum's leadership into feeling that that society was damned and should be abandoned. It also meant, once its hopes of influencing society through legal, democratic means such as political campaigns were wrecked, that if Asahara's contention that spiritual action was no longer enough to fulfil its mission were correct, it had to look elsewhere for the means by which to influence or control Japanese society.

Shortly afterwards Asahara summoned followers to the island of Ishigaki in Okinawa in April 1990. He had before predicted that a major earthquake was about to engulf the country and that followers should go with him to Ishigaki to avoid it and take part in a seminar.[17] The event caught the attention of the media and large numbers of journalists followed Aum members to the island, some of them speculating about the potential for mass suicide because of the election debacle. Although the media intrusions caused problems for the seminar, numerous members decided to become renunciates during it. The event also heralded the announcement of a new step forward in Aum's path.

In Ishigaki Asahara announced that Aum had moved forward onto the Vajrayāna path of Buddhism. It would cease to be primarily a Mahāyāna Buddhist movement (in which members strove for the salvation of all beings) but would move to the Vajrayāna path of Buddhism which – in his interpretation – focused more specifically on the salvation of the individual and recognised that not all people were capable of attaining salvation. He saw this move from Mahāyāna to Vajrayāna Buddhism (which focused on tantric and esoteric practices and empowerment through initiation rituals) as a progression to a higher form of religion, one for the special few. As has been noted earlier, such interpretations of Buddhist teaching were Asahara's own, rather

---

16. Young 1995: 232–233.
17. *Shūkan Yomiuri* 1995 6/1 p. 63.

than being standard Buddhist views of things. In this case he seems to have drawn inferences from his readings about Vajrayāna Buddhism that fitted his own needs. In particular it appears that he interpreted the Vajrayāna path of secret initiations as a higher path accessible to only the few, and that he read into it the justification for those at higher stages of development to remove evils by disposing of those at lower stages of advancement.[18]

He further announced that, in order to prepare for Armageddon, an image that had begun to attain increasing prominence in his talks by this time, Aum would embark on a programme of building communes where it could withdraw from the world and pursue its task of saving its own members not just spiritually but physically as well, with Asahara talking of the need to build nuclear shelters so that Aum could protect its members. As Shimazono has remarked, there is a sharp and rapid shift here from the 1988 concept of building Lotus Villages to prepare for the development of the ideal kingdom on earth, Shambala, to the 1990 one of building nuclear shelters to protect the movement.[19] The suggestions made in books such as *Metsubō no hi* that not all humanity could be saved had thus, by spring 1990, developed into the perception that Aum should no longer focus its energies on saving those outside the movement but should turn its attention solely to itself: in the period in which it had experienced public rejection and humiliation, as well as media investigations, and had engaged in violence of its own, Aum had also moved away from seeking a utopia on earth for all, to building defences around itself to protect it against the world and to seeking salvation only for its own followers.

Communes, Conflict and the Perils of Communal Life

From May 1990 onwards Aum began to seek out more rural land on which to build its communes, often doing so through dummy companies that concealed the real name of the buyer. This process brought it into numerous conflicts, both with regional authorities and with local farmers in many parts of Japan who did not want a communal religious group (especially one that had become somewhat notorious due to the Sakamoto, *Sunday*

---

18. Brennan 1995: 385.
19. Shimazono 1995: 36.

Mainichi and election affairs) to set up communes in their neighbourhood. Eventually Aum was embroiled in disputes and court cases wherever it tried to establish communes, both as a result of negative attitudes on the part of the local people and because it showed scant regard for legal processes, frequently putting up buildings without permission, or for local sentiments.[20]

One such case was the Aso affair, where Aum bought 5.9 hectares of land in May 1990 in Namino village in the Aso area of Kumamoto prefecture, and started to clear the land to build a commune. However, in June 1990 the Kumamoto prefectural authorities put a holding order on this work, claiming that Aum infringed the rules, since it had not got permission (as it legally should have, for developments of woodland areas more than 1 hectare large) to carry out this work. Aum issued a suit against the Kumamoto Governor Hosokawa (later Japan's Prime Minister) stating that the land was moorland and hence not liable to this regulation, and became embroiled in numerous legal battles as a result. Although the details of this affair and the various accusations and law suits are too complex to go into here[21] what is perhaps most important to note is that the dispute appeared to strengthen Aum's views that the outside world was hostile to it and ready to prevent it from acting as it wished, and that, as in previous cases of problems, Aum's response here, and in its other disputes with regional authorities and local communities, was to go on the offensive and take an unconciliatory stance.

The legal moves by the state authorities to block its plans were viewed by Aum as an example of state persecution of religions, as was the refusal of local authorities to allow Aum members to register in Namino, because they were fearful that an influx of Aum residents would lead to Aum taking over, via elections, the local council.[22] In fact, the action of the local authorities in refusing to register Aum members as residents was

---

20. See Fujita 1995: 25–27 for a brief overview of such problems and pp. 136–161 for detailed discussions of the Namino and Kamikuishiki cases.

21. Besides Fujita's account there is also a volume on the Namino affair published in 1992 with assistance both from the villagers and from Aum: see Kumamoto Nichinichi Shinbun (ed) 1992.

22. This was a reasonable fear, both in Namino and later at the main Aum commune at Kamikuishiki, for in both cases the number of local residents was small and the number of probable Aum residents would have given the religion a numerical advantage in the community.

illegal and infringed Japanese legal rights to freedom of residence. When Aum took its case to higher courts, it received a judgement in its favour. It received some support from local citizens groups in Kumamoto, who argued that refusing to register Aum members as residents was a denial of the freedom of domicile and a matter of religious persecution.

Despite such victories, Aum encountered continuing problems at Namino: police raids on the commune in connection with the ongoing disputes, in which three Aum members were arrested in October 1990, merely served to intensify Aum's estrangement from the community around it. As a result of these continuing tensions, Aum decided that it would shift the centre of its communal operations to Kamikuishiki in Yamanashi prefecture, where it had been acquiring parcels of land from the latter part of the 1980s onwards. The site at Kamikuishiki became its headquarters and was the place where the sarin was manufactured and where Asahara was eventually arrested.

Here, too, numerous conflicts arose between Aum members and the local community who found the behaviour of the commune conflicted with its own conservative values. Aum members, according to the account given by Fujita Shōichi, often behaved arrogantly and contemptuously towards the Kamikuishiki locals, who were also upset by the constant passage of trucks through the village even late at night, ferrying materials to the commune, and other such inconveniences to their lives. Admittedly the accounts of the Kamikuishiki residents have been brought to us through a sensationalised media filter at present (one assumes that the Kamikuishiki villagers themselves recognise there is no mileage in saying that Aum members were really quite nice neighbours!) but their experiences, which tally with those of the people in Namino, indicate that Aum did not attempt to exist on good neighbourly terms with those around it and that it displayed an inability to compromise in any way or to meet the villagers on any other than its own terms.[23] One of the problems at Kamikuishiki was that Aum acquired its land there piecemeal, and its acquisitions were thus separated from each other. Thus members had to use public roads to move between facilities, and this occasioned increased interaction and conflict with the locals, especially since Aum members often donned

23. Fujita 1995: 135–163.

masks and hoods to shield themselves from the view of outsiders.[24]

Despite winning some of its battles in the courts, the Namino affair – especially when allied to the problems and tensions that developed around its other communes – largely confirmed Aum's feeling that it was being persecuted and stopped from fulfilling its mission. It also demonstrated, however, how ready Aum was to use duplicity to conceal its own actions, through buying land under false pretences, and its contempt for laws that conflicted with its wishes and needs. The move to communal life after the Ishigaki seminar (which itself came close on the heels of the election debacle) thus brought Aum into an escalating cycle of conflicts and tensions, and contributed greatly also to its own escalating cycle of violence.

Communal Living, Hierarchy and Defections

This retreat from the world, besides bringing Aum into more conflicts, court cases, and public disrepute, also intensifed its closed, hierarchic nature and played a major part in narrowing the perspectives of its members and enhancing the authority of its leaders. The hierarchic structure based on ascetic attainment and initiations certified and granted by Asahara gave much power to those at the higher levels of leadership and little to those below them. Miyadai Shinji, for example, reports the testimony of an ex-member who was assigned to work under Murai Hideo in Aum's science and technology programme: when the member asked Murai about the sorts of things being produced there, he was told not to bother himself with such questions as they were not important for him to know.[25]

The rigours of communal life and of the intense ascetic practices members were expected to do meant that members did not have the scope for doubt or for assessing the activities of their religion that someone living in the mundane world might have. It appears that members had fairly limited contacts with their peers: Noda Naruhito noted that one of the codes of conduct for Aum members such as himself was to avoid 'flowery language' (i.e. ordinary talk or chatter) because this was a dissipation of energies

24. See, for example, the photograph of Aum members thus dressed, in Mainichi Shinbun Shūkyō Shuzaihan (ed) 1993: 127.
25. Miyadai 1995: 30.

better utilised in the struggle for enlightenment.[26] These
restrictions blocked the possibility of any checks being made on
the policies of the leaders, and helped make them increasingly
remote and autocratic.

The communal nature of the movement had thus intensified
the power and authority of its leader(s) and made them almost
(inside Aum) unanswerable and led to their wielding draconian
powers over their followers. As yet it is not known how many
members suffered maltreatment in the last few years, but
evidence has emerged that at least one person, Ochida Kotārō,
who had been a long-term member and who was threatening to
leave the movement and denounce Aum because of what he saw
as the failure of its spiritual healing techniques, was strangled in
Asahara's presence, in February 1994.[27]

Thus the communal lifestyle not only served to bring Aum
into greater conflicts with the outside world while cutting it off
from that world's realities, but it also spawned increasing internal
violence. Although the numbers of *shukkesha* increased in 1993-94,
this was, as was noted earlier, due to the immense pressures being
put on members to do so, in order for them to be saved at
Armageddon. Since hierarchy was based on apparent
achievement in ascetic terms (sanctioned by Asahara) and since
members had already bought into this hierarchy, this left little
scope for dissent within the movement. Indeed, as Taguchi's
death in 1989 demonstrates, internal dissent (which could in other
circumstances have been a check on excesses) was not a safe or
viable option: the only path of dissent became complete escape, a
process that in turn became a potential threat to the life of the
movement.

Fujita reports that the number of members leaving
Kamikuishiki increased quite rapidly from mid-1994 onwards,
and whilst he does not provide any figures or names of such
members, the fact that there were numerous ex-Aum members

---

26. *Shūkan Asahi* Oct 13, 1995: 25–6.

27. Ochida had placed his sick mother in Aum's healing facility in Tokyo,
but had become dissatisfied at the failure, as he saw it, to cure her through
spiritual means, and at the expense of the treatment. When he tried to move
her and to leave the group he was strangled, apparently at Asahara's orders.
Asahara has admitted to being present when he was killed, the only case (as
of the present) where he has admitted to any connection to the crimes
committed by Aum. Asahara's wife has also been charged in this case after
admitting that she was present when Ochida was killed.

available to give interviews to the press in the era period after March 1995 suggests that some people had successfully left the movement.[28] Aum made great attempts to bring at least some of them back: often such people were drugged and detained, either at Aum's medical facility in Tokyo or at one of the communes, and at times even incarcerated in containers. A series of criminal charges connected with such activities has since been levelled at numerous members of Aum, including Takahashi Eiko, who was one of its chief nurses at its hospital.[29] Ironically it appears that Aum leaders thought they were helping the escapees by bringing them back: increasingly convinced that the only way to avoid Armageddon was to become a renunciate, they wanted to 'save' their followers by persuading them to come back to the commune rather than return to the everyday world which was heading for destruction.

Nonetheless the apparent loss of members, and the fears that such losses would occur, became a threat to the continued existence of the group. This threat may go some way towards explaining why Asahara's talks began increasingly to talk about external threats, to question the possibility of the movement continuing, and to raise the spectre of a conspiracy against Aum (see below, Chapter Three). The apparent growth of such external threats would help to strengthen and reaffirm his authority inside the movement and increase his control over his followers. Such threats would also, from the Aum perspective, make leaving the movement appear an increasingly dangerous action: the closer and more inevitable Armageddon was, the more dangerous it would be to leave the movement, and the greater the external threat to it, the more important it would be to remain inside it.

The internal tensions and the pressures put on members to renounce the world and yield up their assets to enable Aum to fulfil its purposes, thus led to the violent detention and treatment of recalcitrant members. It also increased conflicts between Aum and the families of its members; complaints filed with the police against Aum and seeking information about the whereabouts of a son or daughter increased as Aum strove to increase the number of renunciates. It also led Aum into confrontations with families

---

28. Fujita 1995: 62 .
29. Takahashi has been charged with confing and assaulting members at Aum's hospital in Tokyo (*Daily Yomiuri* June 15 1995).

whose members had been coerced into making large donations: as the need to prepare for Armageddon increased, the financial needs of the movement appeared to grow apace, and this led to ever greater attempts to acquire resources from wherever it could. There were also a number of cases where offspring who had joined Aum attempted to force one or the other of their parents to join the movement in order to save them at Armageddon.[30]

The Kariya case, which led to the eventual raid on Aum, is one example of how Aum's increasing demands on its members led it into deeper cycles of violence and confrontation. Kariya Kiyoshi was a 68-year-old property dealer, whose sister had become a member of Aum and who had donated considerable sums of money to the movement to help in its activities, and to receive various initiations. By early 1995 she had handed Aum money and property worth 60 million yen (c. US$ 600,000). However, more demands were made of her, and it was suggested that she become a renunciate and donate everything she possessed to Aum. She had by this stage become desperate at the increasing financial demands on her and fearful about what would happen if she refused. Thus she had decided to leave the movement and had been in contact with her brother, who had already been embroiled in disputes with Aum over his sister's donations, to help her. He was apparently planning to get her away from the movement and to try to reclaim her property when, on February 28 1995, he was snatched off the streets of Tokyo and abducted in a rental van. This was traced to Matsumoto Takeshi, an Aum member, whose address was given as Aum's Kamikuishiki commune. Although Aum denied knowledge of his whereabouts, he has since been arrested and charged in connection with the Kariya case and, as we have seen, evidence has emerged since that Kariya was taken to Kamikuishiki, killed and his body disposed of in an industrial microwave oven purchased by the group.

Conclusions to Chapter Two

As this chapter has shown, the period roughly from April 1989, when Aum applied for legal status as a religious corporation, until April 1990, when its seminar at Ishigaki pointed to the

---

30. See Fujita 1995: 164–183 for detailed descriptions of a number of such cases.

movement's increasing communalisation and world-rejection-ism, was a critical period in Aum's history. It was in this period that Aum began to react to external rebuffs with aggressive and ultimately violent responses, and that its millennialism became increasingly catastrophic in focus. This led to further withdrawal from the world into communes which stimulated further tension with the outside world and intensified Aum's introspection. It also led to an increase in internal violence and to an escalation of tension within the Aum community. This process was accompanied by, and encouraged the development of, Asahara's growing concerns about the imminence of Armageddon and its scale, and by an escalating feeling that the outside world was not just hostile to Aum but was actively conspiring to destroy it, and it is to these matters that we shall now turn in Chapter 3.

Chapter 3

Prophecies, Poisons and the Whiff of Conspiracy

The Prophecies of Asahara Shōkō

Although Aum made some attempts to improve its public image in the wake of the problems it ran into in 1989–1990, it failed to increase its following very much in the next two years, hardly recruiting any *shukkesha* at all during 1991 and 1992. This was also a period when Aum ran into increasing difficulties and conflicts with local communities and regional authorities in the areas where it had built its communes or was attempting to establish facilities. Its internal dynamic was thus one in which the movement's sense of mission and its vision of the coming (and necessity) of Armageddon became interwoven with Aum's anger at the world around it, and its growing sense of persecution. Furthermore, Aum's plans for salvation and for the transformation of its renunciates into superhumans who could transcend the horrors of Armageddon were threatened by internal stresses within the movement caused by the escalating drive to acquire resources to prepare for its mission, by the failures of its recruitment activities, and by fears of fragmentation and loss of membership. This was also the period when Aum was becoming increasingly closed as a result of its focus on communal life, and when its hierarchical and authoritarian nature served to increase the powers of Aum's leadership and simultaneously detach it from the mundane realities of the external world, thereby distorting its capacity for balanced judgments.

Although Asahara's prophecies of Armageddon had, from around 1989, become increasingly pessimistic in terms of how much of humanity could survive, and had become more and more focused on the events and the forms in which the pre-millennial catastrophes would occur, they escalated further throughout the 1990s, becoming increasingly infused with dramatic and violent motifs. By 1992, when he gave a series of public lectures at universities throughout Japan, he was predicting that 90 per cent of the world would be killed in the coming Armageddon, a prediction that, by 1994, had been further increased when he prophesied that only Aum renunciates would survive. His teachings, which normally took the form of public lectures or talks to his disciples, taped, transcribed and then published by Aum's own publishing firm, began to manifest both sacrificial and paranoid themes, in which he, and Aum, were seen as facing conspiracies to eradicate them, and in which Asahara became depicted at times as a potential sacrificial victim. Asahara at times resorted to striking Christian images of sacrifice, particularly in his two-volume series *Kirisuto sengen* and *Kirisuto sengen Part 2*, (subsequently published in English as *Declaring Myself the Christ*), where he not only proclaimed that he was the Christ figure, but also likened himself to the Lamb of God who was to be sacrificed for the sake of humanity.

Such images of sacrifice vied, in his rhetoric, however, with the possibilities of confronting the world and resisting that sacrifice – in short attacking the world around Aum, so that, rather than being sacrificed for humanity, he would lead the march to salvation. Both the sacrificial motif and the discussions of his, and Aum's, struggles to save the world and to push his followers towards the liberation that would enable them to survive Armageddon, gradually, also, became overlaid with a profusion of conspiracy theories in which the outside world was seen as plotting to eradicate him and his movement. The themes expressed through such theories reflect what can only appear to be a growing paranoia about the outside world.

As Armageddon, in his prophecies, came closer, his concerns also grew with the forms that it would take, and the types of weapons with which it was fought. This fascination with military matters seems to have become especially pronounced after the 1991 Gulf War, which brought the concepts of high-technology weaponry and of 'surgical killing' to public notice. Certainly

Asahara often mentioned the Gulf War in his sermons, regarding it, it appears, as a testing ground for weapons that might be used in Armageddon, especially by the United States, which figures often in his prophecies as the great enemy which would fight, and extinguish, Japan at Armageddon.

Besides the predictions about the coming of Armageddon and the forms of violence which would result from it, there are numerous other sub-themes within Asahara's later teachings. These include a fascination with his own powers of prophecy, which are constantly reiterated, as are claims of his unerring accuracy in foreseeing the future, a power gained, it was claimed, due to his spiritual prowess and due to his ascetic achievements. His teachings and sermons also demonstrate a recurrent concern with conspiracies which Asahara felt were being formed against Aum in order to eradicate it, and at times express some barely disguised anti-Semitic prejudices. Interwoven with such teachings are recurrent concerns about the state of the Japanese economy and of Japanese politics. To illustrate the general themes within Asahara's prophecies and to give a general flavour of the types of teaching he gave to his followers I shall here outline three representative works published by Aum in the period between 1992 and 1995, *Risō shakai Shambala No. 9* ('The ideal society, Shambala', No. 9), a magazine produced by Aum and containing summaries and discussions of Asahara's teachings and predictions, *Asahara Shōkō, senritsu no yogen* (The frightening prophecies of Asahara Shōkō) (published in 1993) and *Hi izurukuni, saiwaichikashi* (Disaster Approaches the Land of the Rising Sun)[1] published on March 2 1995, only 18 days before the Tokyo attack.

1. *Risō shakai Shambala* [2]

On the first page of this volume there is a caption announcing that 'the messiah who will come at the end of the century will be blind: the Master Asahara Shōkō, as prophesied by Nostradamus' (pp. 1–2). It accompanies a photograph of Asahara, pictures of soldiers in gas masks holding guns, lightning flashes, pictures of earthquake-damaged roads, mushroom clouds and fighter aircraft. Following

---

1.   I understand that this volume is now (as of January 1996) available in an English translation under this title.

2.   Asahara (ed) 1992.

on from this opening Asahara discusses at some length the validity of his prophecies, noting that prophecy is a specific power acquired by holy people such as Jesus, Buddha and of course himself: it is also a power that is gained from ascetic practice and is a crucial aspect of a true teacher and sacred person (p. 4). Having thus asserted the validity of his prophecies (a point he returns to later) he moves on to warn of the imminence of Armageddon, at this stage still prophesied as coming in 1999 (p. 6), and of the numerous political events that are bringing Japan close to it. In particular he warns of a dangerous rightward shift in Japanese and world politics, seeing this as signaling a move towards militarism. He predicts that Japan will be drawn into war by 1994 (p. 64) and warns of the dangers of Japanese troops being sent abroad as part of the UN Peace Keeping Organisation (PKO) forces.[3] He also suggests that there are disturbing parallels between the 1990s and its drift, as he sees it, to the right and towards militarism, and the period immediately prior to World War Two (pp. 9–13). One might perhaps suggest that Asahara's concern with the apparent parallels between the present and the 1930s might also, subliminally, be concerned with the move, in the 1930s in particular, towards rigid state control of religion and to attempts by the state to suppress dissident religious movements, hence reflecting his underlying fears that the state might move against and suppress his own movement.

There are ways to escape Armageddon however, through the spiritual powers that are taught in Aum, which is an organisation of 'superhumans' (*chōjinrui shūdan*) (p. 30). The ability of Aum practitioners to transcend the normal ways of the world and acquire superhuman status is emphasised through discussions of their various ascetic accomplishments such as the underground and underwater demonstrations mentioned in Chapter 1 (p. 32ff). Reference is made to Jesus' three day seclusion (i.e. the period between crucifixion and resurrection) in which he, according to Asahara, attained *samadhi* (enlightenment) and demonstrated his power as a messiah (p. 39). Links are thus drawn between the

---

3. The validity of sending troops overseas in a peace-keeping mission was hotly debated in Japan because of the 'peace clause' of the Constitution which, because of Japan's military past, resolved that Japan would renounce war forever and that bound Japan to not engaging in overseas military campaigns.

spiritual practices which transformed Jesus into a messiah, and the practices accomplished by Aum members.[4] Like Jesus, Aum too will be persecuted: references are made to the Gospel of St. Matthew which, according to Asahara, predicts that the movement that will arise to save humanity will suffer persecution for its actions – as indeed Aum has been persecuted: photographs of newspaper headlines and articles disparaging Aum and telling of decisions made by regional authorities such as the Namino council to not allow Aum members to register there, are printed alongside the page to emphasise this point (p. 38).

There are further reiterations of the coming apocalypse and of the messiah (Asahara) who will lead the way, and of the movement (Aum) that will produce the superhumans who will survive the apocalypse and establish a new kingdom on earth (p. 44). This kingdom will be an everlasting spiritual kingdom, a '1000 year kingdom' (*sennen ōkoku*) that was foreseen in the Revelations of St. John, prophesied by Nostradamus and envisioned also by another seer who, according to Asahara, was endowed with great spiritual power and vision, Adolf Hitler[5] (p. 44). Asahara talks of two ways open to humanity, the way of developing superhuman powers (i.e. the performance of asceticism and renunciation) or the way of the material world. Only the former is a viable option: the latter way leads to over-population, to crises in world food and energy resources, and to disaster (p. 45).

A subsequent section of this volume returns again to Asahara's accuracy as a prophet. We are given a series of his prophecies that have come true (including the right-wing political shift in Japan and the dispatch of Japanese peace-keeping forces abroad, and also a volcanic eruption in Japan) and told that 'Japan is developing in line with the Master's prophecies'(p. 56) – a claim that is repeated in subsequent books.

---

4.   The parallel is thus drawn here between Jesus' seclusion and the underground austerities done by Aum members. One perhaps should just add here that these are Asahara's own interpretations and understandings of Christianity, Jesus and of the Bible.

5.   Asahara appears to have had a fascination for Hitler as a figure of power, in part connected with Hitler's vision of a 'thousand-year Reich', which Asahara seems to have glossed with the prophecies of Nostradamus and of the Revelations for the post-millennial world, and partly, it would appear, because of Hitler's anti-Semitism which (see below) fitted in with the prejudices that came through in Asahara's various diatribes against 'Jewish conspiracies'.

How, we are asked, do Asahara's prophecies work? How can he know the future? The answer, we are told, lies in the very structure of the universe: this present world is but one of three worlds – the causal world, the astral world and this present (material) world – which co-exist. The events of this world are created and are first seen in the causal and astral worlds: the astral world is a realm of sounds and vibrations which are reflected in and made concrete in this world; the causal world is a realm where the underlying factors – the spiritual causes, as it were – of the events are manifested, and this present world is where the traces and impulses of these two worlds coalesce and are manifested. Because of the interrelationship of these three worlds, those who can 'see' into the true nature of the causal and astral realms can perceive, in them, the future of this world. Asahara, then, because of his advanced spiritual powers, is able to view the events of this world as they are created through a combination of causes and vibrations in the causal and astral worlds. The proof of such assertions, we are told, is found in science, and we are shown various diagrams showing the interactions of the three worlds, and of how events in the present, material world are first formed in these other worlds. Since Asahara has acquired the spiritual powers to see beyond this world into the astral and causal realms, he is able to see the future as it will happen: his prescience and prophecies are thus, in such terms, 'scientific' in that they involve the clinical observation of phenomena as they develop in the other realms and the analysis of how they will manifest in the world of phenomena (pp. 56–58).

Two comments are perhaps in order here. The first is that here again, 'science' (as an image) is utilised, as it was in relation to the demonstrations of ascetic power given by Aum members in the late 1980s, to 'prove' the veracity of the movement's claims and of Asahara's spiritual stature. It is of far less importance, in such terms, whether the explanations given of Asahara's powers, or of the ways in which phenomena are produced, can really be proved to be 'scientific'[6], than it is to note that Asahara believed, or at least asserted, that he was able to see into the future and that that future was already a scientifically determined reality. The

---

6.   In reality, of course, it is clear that such an analysis cannot begin to be described as 'scientific' since it rests on an assumption – the existence of the causal and astral worlds – that has not been verified by scientific methods.

second comment is that since Asahara's prophecies were based in his spiritual powers, and since the events of this world are pre-determined and formed in other worlds into which he had direct insight due to those powers, were his prophecies to fail or to not occur as he had stated, it would therefore mean that he could not have seen properly into the astral and causal worlds where the events of this world are formed. In short, if events failed to occur as he said they would it would mean that his spiritual powers were not what they were claimed to be: they would be fraudulent and invalid. In such terms, given that the structure of Aum was built on his attainment of higher states of being to which he guided and initiated his disciples, the failure of his prophecies would undermine Aum completely.

2. *Asahara Shōkō, senritsu no yogen* [7]

This volume is largely a collection of Asahara's talks in spring 1993, along with an editorial introduction which emphasises the unerring accuracy of his prophecies with the words:

> The world is developing as Master [Asahara] predicted (*sekai wa sonshi no yogendōri ni ugoite iru*) (p. 1)

Again we are given a series of his correct predictions, such as the collapse of the Soviet Union, the reunification of Germany, the union of the EC, the dispatch abroad of Japanese peace-keeping forces and the liberalisation of food imports into Japan. Again one notes that the prophecies that have come true are ones that anyone with some political perception might make: one also notes that no mention is made of predictions that went wrong, such as those he made over his 1990 election campaign. By contrast, the prophecies that he makes concerning the future and the fate of the world are of an altogether different type, in which Armageddon and apocalypse are the order of the day: the leap between the levels of events thus predicted is quite striking.

What is especially crucial for the world, according to the editorial introduction, are Asahara's prophecies concerning the end of the world, and in particular his prophecy of the final war of humanity (Armageddon), which will occur, according to Asahara, without fail (*machiganai*) in 1997. It was in this series of public lectures, in March–April 1993, that Asahara first

---

7.   Asahara 1993.

announced that the date of Armageddon would not be in 1999 as originally predicted (and predicted also by some other new religions in Japan) but two years earlier, in 1997. No explanation is given as to why the date has been moved forward. The first mention of Armageddon as occurring in 1997 was made by Asahara in a talk on March 28 1993 in Nagoya (p. 103), and subsequently 1997 became the accepted date for Armageddon. This final war will involve Japan and the USA, in which weapons more devastating than nuclear bombs will rain down on humanity and kill people in vast numbers (pp. 1–2). The world had only four years left before this crisis, during which time Japan would be faced with extraordinary economic turmoil and social unrest. Again, we are warned of the Japanese rush to militarism and the inevitability of war as Japan and the world seem set on a timetable to destruction. The aim of the book is to describe the coming destruction and to warn what is going wrong, while providing those who seek help with an alternative course of action in which they can survive the end of the world (pp. 2–3).

Asahara's talks are full of exhortations to his followers to deepen their ascetic practice as a means of transcending the calamities that are coming. He also displays an increasing tendency not just to talk about the coming of Armageddon, but to reflect on its nature and on the means of destruction that will be used in it, displaying as he does a growing fascination in weaponry, at times fused with wild conjectures about what his potential external enemies are doing. We are thus treated to various discussions of the weapons Asahara thinks are being created to vent destruction on the world, and to discourses about how these have been tried out already in such events as the Gulf War (which in such respects becomes a trial arena for Armageddon). Thus we are told about the development of plasma weapons, which can eliminate humans through destroying their plasma and atomising their bodies, while avoiding damage to property, and are informed that 100,000 Iraqis died in the Gulf War but that only a small proportion of bodies were recovered: most disappeared because they had been atomised by plasma weapons. The Americans, we are told, now have such weapons at their disposal and are preparing to use them at Armageddon.

Armageddon was inevitable and could not be avoided. Its coming, however, was not such a bad thing, for everyone had to face death: to know that one's fate was at hand allowed one to concentrate one's energies on preparing for it, and to focus on passing through the *bardo* (the period of transition after death) properly. In other words, death, and the coming war, were not to be feared but welcomed for the spiritual stimulus they provide (pp. 10–23). It should be added, however, there was a way to avoid being destroyed at Armageddon: to become a superhuman (*shinkajin*) through following Aum's spiritual disciplines and becoming a renunciate.

Although Asahara talks of how to overcome this fate through spiritual power he also occasionally muses about the possibilities of preventing the coming defeat through military means. Despite the concerns he had raised previously about Japan's growing militarism, he also complains about the lack of military preparation and power of the Japanese Self-Defense Forces (*Jieitai*), suggesting (on April 9 1993, at a meeting in Kōchi in Shikoku) that they need to take steps to rectify this and to redress the military imbalance by manufacturing chemical weapons. He even mentions by name one chemical weapon that could be manufactured in this respect – a gas called sarin (p. 124).[8] Asahara's talk of April 9 1993 in Sendai is the first occasion, as far as is known, when this gas, now so closely associated in the public mind with Aum Shinrikyō, was mentioned in public.

The talks in this volume range widely and somewhat chaotically, incorporating a strange admixture of themes, from discussions of Nostradamus' prophecies to assertions of the evil manipulations of the Freemasons (who according to Asahara have destroyed religions and promoted evil in the world) and of the conspiratorial activities of the Jews, who are a recurrent factor in the growing conspiracies Asahara was beginning to see ranged against his religion, interspersed with comments about the Japanese economy, the level of the yen and of stocks and shares. Alongside these are frequent references to the coming of Armageddon, the type of destruction that it will herald, and the importance of the new forms of weapon that will be used in it. We are told frequently that Japan is doomed at Armageddon, but that

---

8. Why sarin in particular caught Asahara's attention is not clear. There may be a link with his fascination with Hitler (see above) since it was the Nazis who originally produced (but did not use) this particular gas. It might also, however, have been because, due to Aum's activities in Russia and to its contacts with ex-military people there, it was able to get the formulae and the materials for making this gas.

there is a way out of this predicament through meditation and spiritual practice. War is, in fact, a step in human progress towards an ideal world (p. 212) and thus Armageddon should be looked forward to with joy because this is when Aum's truth will triumph.

3. *Hi izurukuni, saiwaichikashi*

By 1993, then, Asahara had moved the date of Armageddon from 1999 to 1997, and had begun to be increasingly concerned with, and draw attention to, chemical weapons. He had also begun to talk openly about sarin, and to muse about the importance of making it as a means of defence. By 1995, as this collection of talks and discussions shows, his prophecies and discourses had become still more centred on imminent danger. Aum's rhetoric had become even more focused on the accuracy and inevitability of his prophecies, the coming of Armageddon had been brought even closer to hand, and the concern with weapons and with conspiracies against Aum had become more pronounced. The preface of this book (published, as has been noted earlier, less than three weeks before the Tokyo subway attack) claims that Asahara had, on January 8 1995, predicted that something disastrous would happen around January 18 in Kobe. Since the Great Hanshin earthquake had occurred there on January 17, it was clear, according to Aum, that he had in fact foretold the earthquake (pp. 1–2), further proof, indeed, of the unerring truth of his prophecies. Moreover, the earthquake was not a natural event but one created by a new form of weaponry that caused earthquakes: it was the first blow, as it were, in the final war (1995: 1–2), which thus had started already. Japan was on the very brink of disaster, and there was no time left: the only way out was to become a renunciate. Armageddon had been brought closer yet again: in 1993 it had moved from 1999 to 1997, and in 1995 its starting date moved two years again, from 1997 to 1995. Since Asahara's powers of prophecy were unerring, and based in his spiritual powers which allowed him to see the truth before it happened, it thus followed that Armageddon must necessarily occur, or at least start to manifest itself, in this year, if his claims to spiritual power were not to be severely compromised.

We are informed again of the weapons of destruction that will be used in Armageddon (and in this volume, as in the previous two mentioned, we are given various diagrams and depictions of futuristic weapons), and again we are told of the plasma weapons that will be used to eradicate humanity. However, we are also told of ways to avoid the effects of plasma weapons: through Aum's path of spiritual and yogic disciplines, people can become transcendent beings who cannot be harmed by such weapons (pp. 226–228).

The book also provides us with a summary of various recent natural events and disasters, all of which are linked together as elements in the inevitable progression towards the final end. It contains a strong attack on the mass media, pilloried as a causal factor in the destruction of the world because of its role in promoting base desires and materialistic viewpoints, spreading falsehoods and controlling the minds of deluded people. Alongside these examples of dramatic disturbances in the equilibrium of the world we are provided with various citations from Asahara's speeches over the past years to illustrate his prophetic accuracy and to demonstrate the events that, he prophesies, are now at hand. Thus we hear about the imminent destruction of Japan, the complete eradication of England (p. 318, predicted on January 30 1991), and the certainty of Armageddon in the very immediate future, caused by the increasingly bad karma of the world's inhabitants (p. 322 – prophesied first on March 28 1993, then again on April 17 of the same year and now reaffirmed as being close at hand). There are assertions, too, that one chooses one's own destiny which will determine one's fate during Armageddon – in other words, those who choose to live a correct life by following Aum's precepts will be saved while those that do not, will not, and they therefore in some way deserve to die. We are then given a brief outline of what will follow from Armageddon and the destruction of the corrupt world: the move from destruction to progress, the coming of Christ (i.e. Asahara) and the building of a new civilisation, of 1995 being the great turning point in world history (p. 334), of Aum's mission to build a new world (p. 343), and the advent of a this worldly utopia whose inhabitants would live for an immensely long time (pp. 348–349).

In such terms Asahara's last book that appeared before the subway attack is not just another series of talks, prophecies and exhortations but is a run-through of his past teachings and an attempt to illustrate just how his prophecies fit in with the events of the past few years, and a vision of how events are moving towards the destruction he predicts and, it appears, hopes for. It thus represents a culmination of his teachings and aspirations, perhaps even a final statement of intent and purpose, and an expectation of the fulfillment of his mission.

The Conspiracy to Destroy Aum

There are recurrent motifs running through his books, and through Asahara's thinking in the 1990s. He is concerned about the present direction of the world in general and Japanese society in particular, and this concern is coupled with a growing conviction of the unavoidability of Armageddon, of the need to do ascetic practices as the way to transcend Armageddon when it occurs and to move forward to the new world that will emerge afterwards. There is a recurrent emphasis on the truth and certainty of his prophecies, based as they are on a prescience gained through spiritual practice. As Armageddon comes closer we see a growing tendency to welcome it as a necessary means of removing the evils of this world. Asahara also puts his own credibility, and implicitly his status as a religious leader, on the line by asserting that he is able to see the future due to his spiritual powers, and by outlining not just what that future will be, but increasingly, its timetable. Events that do happen, such as the Hanshin earthquake, are taken to validate this timetable and to affirm the inevitability of what will follow. Increasingly, too, as Armageddon gets closer, one sees a rising interest in the mechanisms of Armageddon and in its weaponry of destruction.

The fascination with destruction and its means, and the increasingly rigid and imminent timetable set for it, are accompanied by another, crucial and escalating theme in Asahara's teachings, that of a conspiracy (or series of conspiracies) being mounted against Aum in order to stop it from its task. The Aum magazine *Vajrayāna Sacca*, in a response to the raids of March 22 1995, published an edition outlining a long running conspiracy against Aum in which, it suggested, poison gases had been used against Aum in the Fujinomiya area (where the Kamikuishiki commune is located) since November 1989.[9] This is an interesting

---

9. *Vajrayāna Sacca* No. 9, 1995 p. 36. On pp. 36–39 of this magazine there is a chronology of the Aum affair as seen through Aum eyes.

date for Aum to have selected as the starting date of the conspiracies against it, as it tallies with the date of the murder of the Sakamoto family. It was not, however, until much later that Aum began to publicly accuse outsiders of conspiring against and attacking it is this way. In October 1993, according to *Vajrayāna Sacca*, the movement had uncovered evidence of attempts to injure its practitioners through the use of this gas.[10] Asahara first publicly stated this 'evidence', according to Aum's own chronology of the affair, on March 11 1994 at Aum's Sendai branch.[11] From this time on the allegation that sarin was being used in attempts to kill him became a recurrent and dominant theme in his talks, repeated, for example, on March 15 1994 in Tokyo (on which occasion he also mused about biological warfare and about the feasibility of developing botulism germs as weapons)[12] and again a few days later, on March 21, in Sendai. Here again he alleged that both he and Aum itself were in grave danger because of sarin attacks, and suggested that the origins of such attacks could be traced back to 1989, since when he and his family had repeatedly been ill because of these attacks on them.[13] There was a widespread conspiracy to destroy his religion and everywhere he went, he alleged, poison gases were spread, usually by agents of the Japanese or American governments.

Aum publications also claimed that from around 1992 its members had started getting ill especially at Kamikuishiki, and that its own searches of the premises (aided by equipment imported from Russia) had detected the presence of sarin in several places, spread around the commune by outsiders.[14] Studies carried out by Aum's own doctors did produce data to show many Aum members living at the Kamikuishiki commune were suffering from various problems (extensive nasal bleeding, blood traces in their phlegm, etc.) that could be attributed to the presence of toxic substances, and these findings reinforced Aum the sense of being the target of a conspiracy.[15] By April 1994, Aum claimed, it had become clear that the American air force planes

---

10. Ibid. p. 37.
11. Ibid. p. 37.
12. Shimosato 1995: 226.
13. Fujita 1995: 61.
14. *Vajrayāna Sacca* No. 9, 1995 p. 37.
15. Shimosato 1995: 217–218.

were dropping poisonous gases on Aum's communes.[16] Evidence of their presence began to appear in Aum publications shortly afterwards: in *Hi izurukuni, saiwaichikashi*, for example, it was claimed that American military aircraft constantly interrupt Asahara's talks with overflights and posed grave threats to Aum: the book also contains photographs of these aircraft.[17]

While the conspiracies against Aum were generally instigated and carried out by the Japanese and American governments, they involved at different times various Japanese religious groups such as Sōka Gakkai, as well as other agencies commonly associated with conspiracy theories, including the Jews and the Freemasons, who are frequently cited as active agents in various world conspiracies planning for Aum's destruction.[18] There are many other evil agents involved in plots to kill Asahara, to undermine Japan, to destroy much of humanity and to seize world power and domination for themselves. In particular Asahara claimed that a vast conspiracy involving Japanese and foreign agents existed to subvert Japan, and to work in tandem with the USA, the Jews and various other agencies for world domination. This conspiracy was 'exposed' in the Aum magazine *Vajrayāna Sacca*, in a special edition in 1994, which not only outlined a Jewish and Freemason conspiracy against Japan, but also published a 'blacklist' of 12 Japanese and two foreigners active in Japan, who were 'wanted' for having 'sold their souls to the devil' as part of the conspiracy. Amongst those named in this context were the Emperor who had long been an agent of the Jews; Crown Princess Masako (the highly popular wife of the heir to the throne, who had spent many years abroad as a student and is fluent in English: she is an agent of American business, and is charged with plans to destabilise and ruin Japanese industry); Ogata Sadako (the respected Japanese head of UNHCR, who is in charge, according to Asahara, of killing refugees); Ōzawa Ichirō (a successful and conspiratorial politician. who has been in-strumental in establishing various coalitions, has played a major part in the realignments of political parties in Japan in the 1990s,

---

16. *Vajrayāna Sacca* No. 9, 1995 p. 38.

17. Asahara 1995: 122–123.

18. Here Asahara merely appears to be recycling some of the more unpleasant aspects and prejudices of Japanese popular culture and youth culture, which are riddled with ideas and prejudices about the Jews in particular, as well as the Freemasons.

and is now leader of the Japanese Opposition in Parliament) who, in the conspiracy for world government, was in charge of subduing Japan; and the popular American talk-show guest and entertainer Dave Spector, who appears frequently on Japanese television.[19]

These conspiracy theories, or variations on them, also permeated Aum's later responses to suggestions that it had had a hand in various incidents involving sarin and other noxious gases: on such occasions, Aum insisted that people conspiring against it had been responsible (see below, Chapter 4). In the aftermath of the Tokyo subway attack, also, it pointed the finger of accusation at its enemies, especially the Japanese government, which had carried out the attack itself, as part of a wider plan to increase its control of society and to legitimate a crack-down on Aum. The edition of *Vajrayāna Sacca* No. 9, published on April 25 1995, is a good example of Aum's responses to the accusations and raids against it: the whole magazine is devoted to the sarin attack, the Kamikuishiki raids and the 'conspiracy against Aum' that these reflect and that, the magazine alleges, was in full swing.

Quite why Asahara had begun to talk so often about sarin (talk that immediately, in some minds linked the movement with the poison gas attacks first in Matsumoto and then in Tokyo) has yet to be fully deciphered. However, some reasonable surmises have been made by various commentators. Shimosato Masaaki, a journalist with some specialist knowledge in the field of toxins and chemicals, has pointed out that Asahara's first discussions of sarin come at approximately the time when (as has subsequently been discovered through police inquiries) Aum was developing its plans to manufacture sarin and to arm itself against the hostile world around it. Its increasing emphasis on sarin as a weapon used against Aum coincided with the growing evidence of illness at Kamikuishiki found by its own doctors. Thus, Shimosato suggests, Aum's experiments at making sarin may at times have gone wrong, and Aum had, therefore, been responsible for the sufferings of its members (the majority of whom were unaware of what their leaders were doing). The accusations of poisoning were intended to explain to Aum members why they were getting ill and to cover up Aum's own conspiratorial activities. Shimosato also suggests that by introducing discussions about sarin and

---

19. See Fujita 1995: 63–64 for a more detailed account of this blacklist.

about conspiracies in which sarin would be used, whilst also planning to make and use sarin, Asahara was also providing a basis upon which his prophecies could be seen to come true, thus further demonstrating his own powers.[20] One might also suggest that such talk of conspiracies was aimed at exhorting the members to intensify their practice, and at heightening the feeling among the membership that it was beleaguered by a hostile world, in order to increase the leadership's control over them, to stop them defecting and to persuade them of the importance of becoming renunciates.

Asahara, in the course of discussing the conspiracies against Aum, also expressed the fear that Aum could not continue in such circumstances. On at least one occasion, in April 1994 in a speech in Sendai, he mentioned the possibility of group suicide as a way out of the predicament.[21] This possibility, however, was not as often or as seriously discussed as the other alternatives: one was to strive as quickly as possible to attain enlightenment and thus transcend the perils of their current situation (an exhortation which, as we have seen, recurred throughout Asahara's talks and which was constantly used to persuade more people to become *shukkesha*). The other alternative was for Aum to take steps to defend itself. In this vein, Asahara's talks became infused with comments about the need for Aum to conduct research to counteract the effects of the poison gases that were being used against it, and of the need for Aum to arm itself against society which was bent on destroying it.[22] In the light of such rhetoric (especially as it was backed up by increasing internal violence and pressure on members) it is not surprising the number of defectors was growing (see above Chapter 2), a factor which conditioned further paranoia, increased the likelihood of defections, and made it more essential that Aum's leaders do something to resolve the situation.

Conclusions to Chapter Three

By mid-1993 Aum had begun to move from discussions of the inevitability and welcome need for Armageddon, to an increasing

---

20. Shimosato 1995: 248–249.

21. Fujita 1995: 62.

22. The conspiracy theories and the discussions of the need for self-defence and for offence are well summed up by Fujita 1995: 60–64.

conviction that it was the target of numerous conspiracies. As this happened, the movement's need for self-protection and for making preparations to confront the society that was oppressing it, grew. Asahara's teachings began to provide legitimations for the course Aum was taking, in terms of appearing to justify taking the lives of others. This was, as has been seen, latent in the *poa* concept (of the ability of the advanced practitioner to transfer his or her merit to the dead) and in Asahara's interpretations of Vajrayana thought (see above, Chapter 2). Such ideas became more strongly expressed still in Asahara's talks, for he began to state that living in the mundane, material world was valueless, and to illustrate his talks with stark images in which the lives of those mired in the material world were seen as having little more worth than those of ants. Such people could thus benefit from a swift death, for this would prevent them from building up more bad karma in this world, and thereby hindering their chances of rebirth.[23] These images, prophecies and legitimations of hostility to the outside world went beyond mere words, however, for, in the period from 1993 onwards, Aum also began to take concrete steps to develop the weapons that had featured in its leader's sermons, and it is to this process, and its repercussions, that we shall turn in Chapter 4.

---

23. See Fujita 1995: 70, for a summary of such comments.

Chapter 4

Preparations and Action
The Road to Kasumigaseki

Preparing for Armageddon

Chapter 3 shows just how hostile Aum had become to the outside world, how threatened it felt by it, how deeply talk of violence and weapons had permeated Asahara's thinking, and how far the movement had gone in asserting the inevitability of the final war. In so doing it had not only become committed to the necessary fulfilment of its prophecies, but had come to welcome that final cataclysm as a joyous event that would demonstrate Aum's triumph. What we know now is that Aum had gone far beyond just words and talk: when Asahara mused about violent ways of solving the predicament the movement found itself in, either through internal violence by group suicide, or external violence through attacking its 'oppressors', a path for which Aum had constructed theological legitimations, he and his cohorts had also taken practical steps to prepare themselves for violence. Aum was not just prophesying turmoil, destruction and Armageddon: it was making practical plans to help bring them about.

The exact time when Aum began to make practical preparations to (in its view) defend itself against its enemies – or to engage in a planned and direct confrontation with the world, as the prosecution in the various Aum trials would see it – is unclear. The evidence so far accumulated places this at some point during 1993, around the time that pressures increased within Aum for members to become renunciates, when the numbers of complaints filed with the police by families of Aum members against the religion began to grow,[1] and when Asahara began to publicly talk about sarin and to bring the date of Armageddon forward.

When, on October 20 1995, the court case began against four Aum members including Takahashi Masaya, who were accused to involvement in the Tokyo subway attack, the prosecution case set out the sequence of events which, it alleged, had led to the attack. According to this outline, Asahara gave the order to start preparations for the manufacture of sarin in March 1993. This was the period when Asahara began to publicly mention sarin gas, and according to the prosecution's outline of its case in this trial, one intention of manufacturing the gas was to fit in with these prophecies, and another was to encourage the destablisation required to bring about Armageddon.[2]

It is possible, however, that preparations could have started earlier. Aum had established a medical facility in Tokyo, and had put together a medical team of qualified doctors and nurses, all of whom were committed Aum members, in 1990. While the hospital itself offered a mixture of healing therapies, ranging from alternative methods and Oriental medicine, to Western-style medicine,[3] it was also used (as we have seen in Chapter 2) as a place where dissident Aum members and others whom Aum sought money from, were confined. Several important members of Aum's medical team have subsequently been found to have been heavily involved in Aum's criminal activities, including Hayashi Ikuo, Aum's top doctor, who

1.   Surveys by the *Asahi Shinbun* of March 31, 1995, and by the *Mainichi Shinbun* March 26 1995 both showed a large number of complaints (the Asahi cited 100, and the Mainichi 60 cases) filed with the police by families with grievances against Aum. Most related to complaints that family members who had joined Aum has since disappeared (i.e. were no longer in contact with their families) or that large sums had been demanded or extorted from them by Aum. The majority of these complaints had developed since 1993 (Fujita 1995: 24–25).

2.   The outline of the case according to the prosecution is given in some detail in the *Asahi Shinbun* Oct. 21 1995, p. 21. It should of course be stressed that this is the case as the state's investigators have reconstructed it. Whilst the case has been built to some degree of information and confessions provided by Aum members in custody, as yet, while the various trials are continuing, there are clearly various points of potential dispute in what the prosecution alleges was the course and the nature of the events leading up to March 20 1995.

3.   The interpretation of illness and the provision of remedies and of healing (often of a spiritual type) are important aspects of the Japanese new religions in general. While many of these movements criticise Western-style medical healing as inadequate (for example, because it is seen as a failing to deal with the spiritual causes of illness) they rarely reject it entirely. Rather, they tend to combine standard, Western and Eastern techniques and their own spiritual healing practices, and many also establish their own facilities which do this. As such Aum's establishment of a hospital was in line with the practices of many other Japanese religious movements.

was one of those who placed the sarin in the Tokyo subway, and Takahashi Eiko, the nurse accused of imprisoning various dissident Aum members and others from whom Aum sought donations, against their will, and with illegally administering drugs to them. Moreover, the Aum hospital and its doctors proved to be one of the conduits through which Aum was able to acquire medicines, drugs and other chemicals that were needed in its experiments: as a medical facility it could order materials and equipment which would have been difficult to otherwise acquire legally on the open market.[4] In other words, given that the Aum medical facility and the movement's medical staff have since been heavily implicated in the carrying out of various illicit activities, and given that the hospital itself had been in existence since the summer of 1990, it is possible that it may have had a role in the plans to develop chemical weapons earlier than 1993. However, the evidence put forward in the trials so far has cited spring 1993 as the date to which direct evidence of Aum's efforts to arm itself can be traced.

According to the prosecution case outline in the Takahashi trial, Asahara's orders to develop chemical weapons were given to Murai Hideo, the Aum official murdered in April 1995, and it was he who played a key role in bringing them to fruition. Murai himself had a scientific background: he had graduated from Osaka University in physics and had done some postgraduate studies before working for Kobe Steel's research department, a position he left after reading some of Asahara's books and attending Aum training courses, to become a member of an Aum commune in May 1989. Murai placed Tsuchiya Masami, an Aum member with a Master's degree in organic chemistry from Tsukuba University, in charge of research into chemical weapons.[5] Tsuchiya, who played a major part in providing Aum with the means to transform

---

4. Fujita 1995: 172.
5. It has been widely speculated in the media that Aum had deliberately set out to recruit people with scientific backgrounds from early on. Since Aum also had a number of members who were either members or ex-members of Japan's Self-Defence Forces (SDF, in Japanese *Jieitai*) it has also been speculated that Aum deliberately set out to recruit people with such military backgrounds, thus implying that it had been intent from the outset on planning chemical attacks and military-style activities. However, there has been no clear confirmation of this alleged 'plan' in the evidence. Judging from the evidence that has come to light so far, it appears more likely that there was no pre-determined plot from the beginning to develop in this way, and that Aum moved into this hostile course of action because of the factors discussed in this report. The fact that it had within it people who had some of the technical know-how necessary to be able to put these ideas into practice might in itself have been a factor in the process of putting Aum on a war footing, and in its growing interest in chemical and other such weapons.

Asahara's predictions and plans into reality, was arrested while hiding in an underground room at Kamikuishiki on April 26 1995, along with Endō Seiichi, another leading member closely connected with Aum's criminal activities, and he now faces various charges connected with the affair.

Murai was in overall charge of acquiring the raw materials and equipment needed for Tsuchiya's experiments. During 1993 Aum, which had already become skilled at setting up dummy companies to conceal its identity when purchasing land for its communes, established a number of additional front companies through which it was able to operate. Amongst the companies so established were ones that were used to purchase chemicals, dynamite and items of laboratory equipment, all of which were used in Aum's experiments to make chemical and biological weapons.[6] Other equipment purchased in a similar fashion included the industrial microwave that Aum installed at Kamikuishiki and that was used, according to confessions made to investigators, to dispose of the body of Kariya Kiyoshi after he had been kidnapped and killed at the end of February 1995. From July 1993 onwards, according to the prosecution case, laboratories began to be built at Kamikuishiki: certainly this was a period when a rapid growth in the facilities there was noticed by local residents.[7]

---

6. The production of sarin itself was not technically illegal in Japan at the time: although banned by international conventions after World War Two it had apparently never been formally banned in Japan, largely because it had never crossed the minds of legislators that anyone would ever want to make it. Legislation has subsequently been rushed through the Japanese parliament to make its production illegal. The details of Aum's business dealings and the ways in which they set up dummy companies which concealed their connections to Aum, and the ways in which they acquired various materials, as well as the complexities of the process of making chemical weapons, are rather too technical to go into here. Among the companies established by Aum was the Hasegawa Chemical Company (set up on April 2 1993), which commenced buying in materials that Tsuchiya needed in his experiments, from June 1993 onwards (*Asahi Shinbun* Oct. 21 1995 p. 21). Shimosato 1995 provides details of the processes and materials required to make sarin while Fujita 1995: *passim*, gives information on the companies Aum established: for example, it set up a company named Belle Epoch, registered in Shizuoka prefecture, in August 1993, and at the same time the company Mahapōsha, established by Aum and which had opened computer shops in several Japanese cities, expanded its activities (pp. 50–52).
7. *Asahi Shinbun* Oct. 21 1995. Fujita 1995: 152 gives a list of the various facilities at Kamikuishiki and notes that these had mostly developed since 1993.

A vital factor in this process was Aum's expansion into Russia in 1992. As yet the Russian aspects of the Aum affair have been barely researched[8] and hence there are currently many grey areas concerned with such questions as how it managed to establish a foothold there and to apparently gain more converts there (media reports have generally put the figure at around 30,000 followers) than it had managed to do in Japan. Given the successes of other millennialist movements in the turbulent period since the collapse of Communist rule in Russia, it is perhaps not surprising that Aum was able to develop there too. It also had the advantage of having plenty of money with which to bankroll its activities and to purchase broadcasting time on television and radio. There have been suggestions, too, that it was able to establish itself in Russia readily and to receive favourable treatment from the authorities (or at least to get the authorities to turn a blind eye to its activities) because of its generous use of funds which helped establish political connections with important figures in Russia, including, it has been alleged, Boris Yeltsin.[9] Despite this supposed protection Aum became the target of severe criticisms especially from established religious bodies, and from ex-members with grievances against it, and thus came under investigation by the authorities in Russia before the March 1995 incidents, and ultimately, in March 1995, was proscribed there. Its connections there did, however, allow Aum to gain access to the vibrant Russia black market and to gain access to various materials and hardware, as well as, it has been suggested, formulae for the production of chemical weapons.[10] Thus its Russian links played a central part in Aum's development of a

---

8. There have been a few magazine articles in Japan but as yet (at least in early 1996) no full academic study or account of Aum in Russia.

9. In particular these suggestions centre on Oleg Robof, who had close ties to Aum serving as head of the Japan–Russia Friendship Society established and funded by Aum. Robof, a politician, has been described as being close to Yeltsin (Shimosato 1995: 238, Fujita 1995: 47) and as having been the conduit for several million dollars worth of Aum funds channeled into Russia to establish the movement there, including setting up radio and television stations (Fujita 1995: 47–48). On Aum and Russia see also *Aera* 1995, No. 23, 5/25, pp. 35–37. One should stress, however, that much of what has been reported so far about Aum in Russia has been based on second-hand reports relayed by journalists, and that this area , more perhaps than any other in the whole affair, remains open to speculation and in need of serious academic research.

10. It has been suggested, for example, that Aum produced sarin gas based on Russian formulae and that evidence of this connection was found during the March 22 raids at Kamikuishiki (Fujita 1995: 19).

military capacity. Whether the move itself was taken for such reasons, or whether, having made a successful entry into Russia, Aum found it had access to these materials, and thus was in possession of the means to transform its fantasies into fact, is as yet unclear, and this is one of the many aspects of the whole affair that will require further research, and which may thus influence future interpretations of it.

In 1993, too, according to the Takahashi indictment, the plans for an act, or acts, of mass-destruction (such as the alleged plot, mentioned in the Introduction, to spray sarin from a helicopter over Tokyo) began to coalesce. Hayakawa Kiyohide, who was in charge of Aum's construction activities, arranged for the purchase and import from Russia, through one of Aum's companies, of a Russian MI-17 helicopter, which was capable of carrying large payloads of up to 30 people. The helicopter arrived at Kamikuishiki in June 1994. At the same time that preparations for buying the helicopter were put in motion in 1993, Kibe Tetsuya, another member of Aum's upper echelons, was sent to the USA to undergo training so he could get a helicopter pilot's licence.[11]

Such preparations were, as far as can be ascertained, secret from the main membership of the movement. Since Aum was engaged in various business ventures that were public (such as a computer business run under the aegis of its company Mahapōsha) it was able to use these as a shield for its illicit activities. Although the frequent delivery of materials and the rapid building activities going on at Kamikuishiki could hardly be unnoticed by residents at the commune, its command structures (as well as the growing tensions there) did not encourage any direct inquiries from ordinary members or responses from their leaders. The case of the man who raised questions with Murai Hideo about his tasks at the commune, only to be told to get on with his work and not ask questions (see above, Chapter 2), may well have been typical. In the aftermath of the March raids on its premises, Aum spokespeople explained the presence of huge stockpiles of chemicals as being necessary to make fertilizers or for use in its business activities making computer chips. Such 'explanations' could plausibly have been used earlier to quell the curiosity of commune members. Asahara had begun to talk of the 'secret work' of the movement during 1993–1994. According to

11. *Asahi Shinbun* Oct. 21 1995: p. 21.

the indictments, he informed his leading aides individually of what this work was and how it was being accomplished, during the early part of 1994,[12] but ordinary commune members seem to have been kept in the dark as to what was actually going on at Kamikuishiki.[13] Given the atmosphere around the commune because of the apparent conspiracy, increasingly outlined in Asahara's talks, against Aum and of the imminence of Armageddon, it is perhaps not surprising that many commune members did not openly question what the nature of this 'secret work' was, or that they assumed it involved Aum's preparations for the Armageddon that they knew was soon to come.

Success and Failure

Tsuchiya's team was successful in making sarin in late 1993. They reported to Murai that the plans to produce the gas in some quantity were going forward, and by July 1994 Murai was able to tell Hayakawa that Aum would soon be in possession of large quantities of sarin. The research team's activities did not, however, always go smoothly, and a number of incidents in which gases escaped from Aum facilities drew unwelcome attention to the movement. In July 1993, for example, local residents complained to the police of foul-smelling gases in the vicinity of an Aum facility at Kameido, in Tokyo: although the police attempted to investigate, they were refused entry by Aum officials claiming that this attempted intrusion represented police interference.[14] Here

---

12. *Asahi Shinbun* Oct. 21 1995 p. 21: according to this report, he told leading followers about it in early 1994, i.e. sometime after the plans to make sarin had been activated and the laboratories built . Which people knew for certain what was going on before this time is a little less clear, although it is clear that certainly Murai and probably Hayakawa were in the know from the outset.

13. Given that the Aum facilities at Kamikuishiki were scattered around the region on a number of plots of land, it was relatively easy for the leadership to keep members away from the plot of land and buildings where the sarin laboratories were located.

14. Subsequently, television footage of this incident has been broadcast numerous times in Japan, and questions have naturally been asked about why the police were not prepared to force the issue and gain access to the building. The problem is that the relationship between religions and state agencies such as the police is a very delicate matter in Japan because of the country's pre-war experiences, when the police were used to suppress religious groups, and when religious repression helped strengthen the powers of the state. The result has been that in the post-war era the police have tended to tread very warily in any cases where religions are involved, as this particular incident demonstrates, and to be extremely careful not to do anything that might breach the protection now afforded to religions from state interference.

Aum responded to external difficulties, as it had done ever since its application for legal status under the Religious Corporations Law had run into trouble in April 1989, by going on the offensive, accusing outsiders of attacking it, and by interpreting any external attempts to regulate, investigate or criticise what it was doing, as hostile acts aimed at curtailing its rights or as parts of a conspiracy devised to destroy it. As has been seen earlier, Aum began, in this period, to allege it was being targeted by hostile external agencies that were bombarding it with poisons and to cite cases of its members who had shown signs of sickness as a result. The likelihood, of course, is that whatever poison-related afflictions members suffered in this period were the result of the movement's own experiments and due to substances escaping from them, and that the allegations of external conspiracies to poison Aum members were in part at least conditioned by Aum's need to cover up this fact.

The most dramatic incidence of such gas escapes, however, occurred one year after the Kameido incident, in the region of Aum's buildings at Kamikuishiki, on July 9 1994. On this occasion complaints were made to the police by numerous villagers in the region, who also reported seeing Aum members rushing from one of the commune's buildings wearing gas masks. Soon afterwards the trees, leaves and grass in the area where this emission was said to have occurred showed signs of serious and unnatural damage, suggesting that they had been affected by a noxious substance of some form or other in the vicinity. Since this incident occurred only a short time after sarin gas had been used publicly, with lethal effect, in the central Japanese town of Matsumoto, in Nagano prefecture, the prefecture adjacent to Yamanashi, where Kamikuishiki is located, it raised suspicions in many quarters that Aum was somehow involved in that incident as well.

Mobilisation and Attack: the Matsumoto Affair

On the evening of June 27 1994, at around 10.40 p.m., clouds of gas, subsequently identified as sarin, enveloped the Kita-Fukashi district of Matsumoto in central Japan. In all seven people died and hundreds were injured, some severely: a number of the victims remained in a coma many months later. Shortly after the incident, the police arrested a local man, Kōno Yoshiyuki, whose wife was one of those who were so badly afflicted by the gas that she remains in a coma. Although Kōno had been the first to raise the alarm on the evening in question, he came under suspicion because he was a gardener who had some chemical fertilizers in his possession. The police in a small town with a low crime rate were unable to fathom the incident before them, and ill-equipped with scientific knowledge, they opted for the easy explanation that Kōno had somehow tried to mix up a chemical fertiliser and had thus created a dangerous reaction.

Although Kōno's name was not officially cleared until many months afterwards,[15] there was widespread scepticism about the official police line, for it was felt by those with some scientific knowledge that it was impossible to create sarin either inadvertently or even deliberately just using the types of chemicals Kōno had in his possession for horticultural purposes. Moreover, as the journalist Shimosato Masaaki argued, the mechanics of producing sarin were such that it would have required an organisation to put it into effect: in short, rather than the misguided adventures of a lone gardening enthusiast, the Matsumoto poisoning had to have been a deliberate and organised attack carried out by a group which had the means to manufacture sarin and the motivation to use it.[16]

That there was an organisation with the means to make sarin is of course now common knowledge. Aum also had a motive: it was involved in a court case shortly to be tried in Matsumoto, concerning property it had acquired to build a training centre. The vendor had been kept in the dark about the real identity of the purchaser and when he found that it was Aum, he had sought to have the sale annulled. The case was about to go to trial and Asahara, according to the testimony of some of those now accused of the Matsumoto attack, feared that the judges in the case would rule against Aum. In order to prevent this happening, he ordered the attack, which was carried out in the vicinity of the place where the three judges involved in the case were then residing. The preparations for the attack were organised by Murai, and

15. It was not until well after the March 1995 raids and the evidence they turned up, and not until Aum members had confessed that they had carried out the Matsumoto poisonings, that the police officially exonerated Kōno and publicly apologised to him in July 1995.

16. For a full discussion of such issues see Shimosato 1995, esp. pp. 73–84. He shows that one of the most important chemicals required in the process of making sarin is not normally or legally available in Japan, and argues convincingly that the incident had to be the responsibility of an organisation – which he eventually identified as Aum Shinrikyō.

involved a number of refrigerated trucks fitted with spraying mechanisms, which were driven up from Kamikuishiki to Matsumoto, where the gas was released. The plan was successful in one respect: the three judges in the case were injured in the attack and the case was postponed. As of January 1996 the case remains unresolved.[17]

While one might speculate that, by this time, Asahara might have wanted to test out how effective the sarin his scientists had made really was, there seems to have been little or no sense that this particular attack was part of any coordinated scheme to bring about Armageddon or to spread fear and unease through society. If the accounts that have emerged so far from the Matsumoto case are accurate, it would appear that the use of sarin here was pragmatic and based in the immediate need of heading off this particular court case. If that is so (and so far this explanation is the only one that had been publicly aired in the court cases or confessions) then it appears to have been based in a reaction not dissimilar to that of Aum's leaders when confronted with the inquiries of Sakamoto Tsutsumi, i.e. one that was rather excessive in relation to the actual situation. It was also a response to an immediate problem, and with no real consideration given to its potential consequences. Again, however, just as in the Sakamoto case, Aum evaded immediate detection in the Matsumoto affair, with the suspicion being directed at Kōno Yoshiyuki instead.

The Alternative Government: Mobilising for Armageddon

At the time of the Matsumoto attack, in summer 1994, the movement took the final step in its growing estrangement from and rejection of Japanese society. Aum declared that, because of the need to defend itself against attacks, and in order to prepare for Armageddon and its aftermath, it was establishing its own government structure, complete with various ministries, under the command of Asahara. With the establishment of this 'government' Aum was in effect setting itself up as a state within a state, and placing itself in direct and explicit opposition to the

---

17. This account of the affair is taken from reports of the trial of Nakagawa Tomomasa, formerly a 'minister' in Aum's alternative government, who is charged with participation in the Matsumoto and Tokyo attacks (*Asahi Shinbun* Internet service, January 1996). Nakagawa has admitted his involvement in the Tokyo and Matsumoto attacks although he has so far qualified this involvement by stating that he was not central to the plot and was following orders rather than actively participating in a conspiracy.

existing state and government structure of Japan. The formation of this alternative government was, according to later newspaper reports, carried out just prior to the Matsumoto attack which was thus seen by its perpetrators, as 'the new nation's first act of war.'[18]

The new 'state' consisted of 22 ministries and agencies,[19] under the leadership of Asahara Shōkō, who was titled the *shinsei hōō* (which could be translated as 'sacred emperor' or as 'sacred master of the law' – titles which reflect the theocratic notion that political and religious rule are one and the same). The leading members in Aum's hierarchy were placed in charge of these various ministries. Murai Hideo was in charge of the largest of all, the Science and Technology Ministry, which had around 300 members assigned to it. Hayakawa was in charge of the Construction Ministry, Endō Seiichi (the man arrested along with Tsuchiya) was in charge of Health and Welfare, Nakagawa Tomomasa (now on trial charged with involvement in the Matsumoto and Tokyo attacks) in charge of the Household Agency of the Supreme Master of the Law (*Hōō Naichō*), Hayashi Ikuo in charge of the Medical Healing Ministry, Niimi Tomomitsu in charge of Home Affairs, and Jōyu Fumihiro in charge of Public Relations. Various aspects of Aum's 'work' came under the auspices of its different ministries and agencies. Murai's Ministry of Science and Technology, as has been seen, oversaw the weapon building and chemical warfare programmes, with help and back-up from Hayakawa's and Endō's ministries. Niimi's and Inoue's ministries, along with Hayashi's, also dealt with recalcitrant members and were involved in abducting and bringing them back to the movement.

There are four especially striking things about Aum's alternative government structure. The first is that in many respects it mimicked the established structures of government, showing that whatever alternative or new society Aum offered, it

---

18. These words are Hardacre's (1995: 17), and are based on a report in the *Asahi Shinbun* of August 8 1995.
19. The detailed chart set out in *Shūkan Yomiuri* (1995 6/1: 50) gives 22 main subdivisions directly under Asahara's head office, and it is on this list that I have largely relied. Of these 15 are 'ministries', suffixed by the Japanese ideogram *shō* (ministry), 5 are 'government offices' (*chō*), one is a bureau (*kyoku*) and one an 'institution' (*in*) charged with managing economic affairs. The use of these terms (ministries and agencies) was discontinued in May 1995 after the arrest of Aum's main leaders.

was not all that dissimilar in terms of organisational structure to the one it aspired to replace. The second is that it hinted at Asahara's own imperial aspirations, not only in granting himself emperor-like titles, but in creating household agencies (the *Hōō Naichō*) akin to the Imperial Household Agency (*Kunaichō*) of the official government structure. The third is that, in contrast to governments in Japan, which have a pronounced bias towards gerontocracy, the oldest person put in charge of a 'Ministry' (and hence entrusted with organising society after Armageddon) was Hayashi, who was 48 years old. The youngest were Asahara's eldest daughter (aged 16, in charge of the Communications Ministry) and Inoue Yoshihiro (in charge of the Ministry of Intelligence) who was 25: the average age of Aum's ministers, including Asahara, was approximately 32.[20]

The fourth striking feature is simply that, in so establishing this 'government' Aum was, in many respects, taking the final step along the path of despair at the state of contemporary society and was expressing its ultimate hostility to the status quo. This was the culmination of Aum's withdrawal from and rejection of society, which had started in earnest after its own rejection by that society at the ballot box. By explicitly implementing a structure which affirmed its right to run its own affairs, and which explicitly gave Asahara a theocratic role, Aum was not just cutting its ties with society, but was expressing open opposition to the constitutional bases upon which post-war Japan had existed, i.e. a constitutional democracy in which the Emperor reigned but did not rule and in which the separation of religion and the state was guaranteed. By rejecting such things, and by affirming that it had to establish its own government in order to defend itself against the existing order, Aum was in effect entering into open confrontation with the state and hence going to war with the forces of law and order.

Suspicions and Accusations: the Path to Kasumigaseki

Shortly after the formation of Aum's own government, and after the Matsumoto attack, Aum came into the spotlight because of the gas emission at Kamikuishiki on July 9 1994. At the time Aum

---

20. In calculating the average age I have omitted Asahara's third daughter (aged 12) who is listed as being in charge of a further Imperial Household agency, and who is Asahara's chosen successor as leader.

'explained' the incident, and the presence of toxic gases around its compound, by accusing the Japanese government and its co-conspirators (particularly the American airforce) of having dropped the poison onto Aum facilities.[21] Extraordinarily, there was apparently little further follow-up in this case, nor indeed any immediate link drawn between the presence of poisonous gases in or around the compound of a religious organisation whose leader had publicly talked about sarin gas and had displayed a great interest in it and its properties, and the use of that gas in a town within relatively easy access of Aum's headquarters, and where a court case involving Aum was due to be heard.[22]

However, it appears that by November 1994 the police had begun to tie the Kamikuishiki and Matsumoto incidents together and to have identified the gas in the Kamikuishiki case as being the same as that used in Matsumoto.[23] The link between the two cases was made public in January 1995 through a number of articles in the press. On January 1 the *Yomiuri Shinbun*'s lead article stated that there had been an incident at Kamikuishiki in Yamanashi prefecture in July 1994 in which trees and other vegetation had been damaged, that sarin had been identified as the gas responsible, and that police were examining the possibility of links between this case and the Matsumoto poisonings.[24] The *Asahi Shinbun* followed this up on January 3 1995 with an article noting that Kamikuishiki was where Aum Shinrikyō had its headquarters, and that there had been a lot of trouble between the local residents and Aum there. Thus, over the New Year period – a time when there is normally little news, when newspapers are hungry for major news items and when such stories can attract a great deal of attention – two of Japan's most widely read and respected newspapers had between them publicly linked Aum, albeit indirectly, to the Matsumoto case.

21. Fujita 1995: 66.

22. According to Shimosato 1995: 211–212 the police were aware of Asahara's interest in sarin gas before January 1995. Quite why the police failed to investigate this aspect of the case is (like its apparent failures over the Sakamoto affair) one of the many serious questions as yet unresolved in the affair.

23. Shimosato 1995: 207.

24. Shimosato (1995: 207–209) states that this information was leaked to the *Yomiuri Shinbun* by the police.

Aum's response was to issue writs for libel against the *Asahi Shinbun* over its article, and to also accuse a local factory owner of being responsible for making sarin and using it against Aum.[25] Subsequently, too, Aum spokespeople went further on the offensive complaining that its compounds had been under constant attack from all manner of hostile forces for several years. As we have seen, also, Aum leaders repeatedly accused the American and Japanese governments and their military forces of bombarding Aum with sarin.

Despite Aum's denials, there was mounting suspicion in journalistic circles that the authorities would shortly move against Aum. Shimosato reports that he had heard such talk ever since the Yomiuri article had appeared on January 1 1995: he himself speculated that the authorities would wait until after the forthcoming elections, in April 1995, before conducting a raid on a religious movement.[26] However, the police eventually did not wait so long, perhaps because of the Kariya kidnap case of February 28 1995, which had been quite directly linked to Aum because of Kariya's public dispute with the movement and due to the evidence acquired at the scene of his abduction.[27]

There is some evidence that the raids that eventually took place on March 22 had already been planned prior to the subway attack, and that Aum was aware that they were about to occur. Such suspicions have been fed by media speculation that Aum was tipped off by some of its own members who were in the

---

25. Shimosato 1995: 213 cites local residents as saying that the factory in question had been the source of some local aggravation because of its polluting effects, but that there was never any suspicion in anyone's mind that, while it might have been environmentally unfriendly, it was ever engaged in any illegal activities.

26. Shimosato 1995: 238–239. This line of speculation further affirms the very delicate nature of the relationship between the state and religion: one presumes that the reluctance to move before the April elections was due to government fears that a raid on a religious movement (even one as extreme and unpopular as Aum) would cause it embarrassment if it failed to show any evidence of Aum's complicity in the Matsumoto case. One of the government's leading opponents is the religious movement Sōka Gakkai, which is a major supporter of the main Opposition party, Shinshintō, and this movement (whose leaders had been incarcerated by the Japanese government during the war years) has always been quick to react to any hint of what it sees as state interference in religious matters.

27. One of Aum's rivals, Kōfuku no Kagaku, which claims it was one of its members who recognised the abductors of Kariya as Aum members, used this incident to its own ends, conducting highly visible campaigns to 'save Kariya' from Aum in March 1995 (Astley 1995: 373)

Japanese *Jieitai* (Self Defence Forces), units of which were supposed to have been put on alert at this time, and that it knew that raids on its premises were imminent. According to Shimosato, however, the source of such information might well have been the police or the media for, according to his account, he had heard of the impending raids on or around March 17 1995. On that day, he states, the police leaked news to various media agencies that they would conduct investigations at the Aum headquarters at Kamikuishiki on March 20, and that around 2,000 police would be deployed in this operation. Shimosato further describes how journalists from numerous media organisations prepared to make their way to Kamikuishiki to cover the raids, and tells how he was contacted by a colleague on the staff of *Shūkan Gendai* (a weekly magazine) who was, on the night of March 19, waiting up at Kamikuishiki for the raids to take place the next day.[28]

The implication of Shimosato's account is that the raids on Kamikuishiki had already been prepared before the subway attack took place: indeed, the very size and scope of them, and the obvious need for pre-planning that went into them, lends testimony to such an implication. The further implication of this account, of course, is that Aum's attack on the subway on March 20 was, like the Matsumoto attack, very much an ad hoc action, designed, like Matsumoto, to head off an event that would be detrimental to Aum's interests. It is also possible that Aum's leaders were in part reacting to police action in Osaka on the previous day, for on March 19 police had entered Aum premises in Osaka and arrested three Aum members in connection with the alleged abduction of a recalictrant member against his wishes.

In Aum's subsequent interpretation of events, the period from around February 28 1995, when Kariya Kiyoshi was abducted and when some very direct suspicions of Aum's involvement in this affair began to be publicly aired, heralded a new phase in Japanese society's assault on Aum Shinrikyō, an assault in which, inter alia, the media and Sōka Gakkai played a part.[29] The Osaka incident of March 19, according to *Vajrayāna Sacca*, represented an attack on the religion in which it was the police, not Aum, who were the kidnappers: it was part of this

28. Shimosato 1995: 239.
29. *Vajrayāna Sacca* 1995 No. 9: 38–39.

ongoing 'anti-Aum' campaign.[30] An Aum broadsheet produced in Osaka and handed out on the streets of Kyoto and Osaka in late March, was even more virulent, stating that an Aum member named Inami Satoru had been abducted by the police from an Aum religious centre in the city in the middle of his religious austerities. Drawings of an Aum member in meditation posture being carried off by a group of large policemen adorned the broadsheet, which also carried a furious attack on the 'media lies' which had implied that Aum had kidnapped one of its ex-members. Rather, the broadsheet claimed, Inami's religious freedoms had been infringed by the state, and it angrily demanded his release.[31]

Whether as a reaction to the Osaka incident, or because it expected to be raided itself and wanted to issue a response to the police investigations, or for some other reason that has yet to surface clearly, Aum carried out a further sarin attack of its own on March 20. On that morning ten highly placed Aum members boarded five different subway trains in pairs at various stations in Tokyo.[32] Amongst those involved were some of Aum's 'government' ministers such as Hayashi Ikuo and Nakagawa Tomomasa. The attackers all punctured, with umbrellas, the bags of sarin wrapped in newspaper that they were carrying as they alighted from the trains. The station most badly hit was Kasumigaseki, and its choice appears, to the detached observer, to be deliberate, especially in the light of the suggestion made above, that Aum was aware that it was about to be raided on or around March 20, and that the Tokyo poisoning was designed to deal with an immediate problem, rather than a part of a longer-term strategy. Kasumigaseki station is at the heart of the area in Tokyo where many Japanese government offices are located. More specifically it is where the National Police Agency's headquarters are located, and since the gases were released to coincide with the arrival of trains at the station at the time when people would be arriving for work, it has been widely assumed that the intent was

---

30. Ibid., p. 39.

31. Shūkyō Hōjin Oumu Shinrikyō (n.d.) *Rachi shita no wa keisatsu!*, handed out in late March in Kyoto and Osaka. I am grateful to Kathy Scott for getting a copy of this broadsheet and passing it on to me.

32. *Asahi Shinbun* June 7 1995, p. 1, has a detailed account of the members involved, where they boarded their trains, and where they alighted.

to strike directly at the police force and at those who were conducting investigations into Aum.

The results were that 12 people eventually died from the fumes and thousands more were incapacitated, while the incident itself, and the dramatic pictures of members of the public stumbling coughing and choking out of the station, or being carried away on stretchers, led to the explosion of media stories about Aum that shortly followed. Two days later, as has been described at the beginning of this report, massive raids, ostensibly in connection with the Kariya case, but in reality closely linked – as the gas masks and canaries demonstrated – to sarin, took place.

The raids were not the end of the affair, however. Shortly afterwards, on March 22, Asahara broadcast a pre-recorded message from Aum's Russian base, in which he stated that the time had come for his followers to put into action the plans for salvation and to face death without regret.[33] Subsequent violent incidents followed that were later attributed to Aum (and to which Aum members later confessed) including the attempted assassination, on March 30 1995, of Police Chief Kunimatsu, the head of the National Police Agency (he was seriously injured but returned to work some months later), a series of other gas attacks on trains in the Tokyo-Yokohama area (none of which caused extensive injuries), an attempt to release cyanide at Shinjuku, Tokyo's busiest station, on May 5 1995, which was only just foiled, and the posting of a bomb to the Tokyo Governor's office (it injured an aide) on May 16, shortly after Asahara's arrest. The media also reported endlessly on various Aum plots and ideas that were alleged to have been considered by its leaders, including the aforementioned sarin attack by helicopter over Tokyo, and plans to assassinate prominent religious leaders such as Ikeda Daisaku of Sōka Gakkai and Ōkawa Ryūhō of Kōfuku no Kagaku.[34]

After March 20 1995 Asahara attained the attention and status he perhaps sought for himself through his various claims and public pronouncements. For the next eight weeks he was sought by the police but remained at liberty. During that period, he became, in effect, the single most powerful figure in the

---

33. This tape was first broadcast on March 22 1995, but has been repeated endlessly in Japan since.
34. *Asahi Shinbun* June 19 1995.

country, not just holding centre-stage in the nation's media but able to exert an influence over the general public. This was demonstrated by the immense attention given to such pre-taped broadcasts as that mentioned above, made on March 22, and perhaps even more starkly by the effects of his continuing prophecies which were relayed through Aum broadcasts and tapes at the time. In one of these Asahara (much as he had, in January, predicted that January 18 would be a dangerous day for Japan, especially in the Kobe area) predicted that April 15, a Saturday, would be one of grave significance for Japan and particularly for Tokyo and the Shinjuku area. Fears that Aum had planned another terrorist attack of some sort meant that everyone did what they could to avoid having to go into Tokyo or use its stations. Shops and markets remained closed and the city was abnormally quiet. Shinjuku station – normally a relentlessly buzzing hive of activity thronged with thousands of commuters – was silent and deserted. Asahara's prophecy had in a way come true: something extraordinary had happened on that day: the city had been quiet and Shinjuku silent. In his career of making extravagant claims about his own powers Asahara had perhaps for once succeeded in influencing not just the small band of his followers, but a wider audience, indeed the whole country.

Since Asahara's arrest, the focus has shifted to the trials, many of which are now under way, and to discussions about how to deal with Aum and its remaining members. In December 1995 the government ordered the disbandment of Aum under the provisions of the Subversive Activities Prevention Law, and began moves to strip it of its assets (which, it is intended, would be used to compensate the victims of its crimes). The religion itself is not, however, finished: although Asahara is in prison he continues to inspire faith in some of his followers, who remain convinced that apocalypse is imminent and that the movement has been the victim of a conspiracy. Asahara himself and his leading aides remain in prison facing, at the very least, a long series of trials in which many of them, including Asahara, could receive the death sentence. The path that started with his practice of yoga and a fascination with the acquisition of superhuman spiritual powers, has thus ended in prison, and with the disbandment of the movement he founded.

Concluding Comments to Chapter Four

The summary of Asahara's prophecies and teachings, in Chapter 3, painted a picture of a movement beset with conflicts with the outside world, a growing concern about internal collapse, and an escalating paranoia coupled with a conviction that destruction is close at hand. His talks had become infused with the notion that the time when Aum would have to make its stand against the wider world (either by the course it did choose, i.e. externalised violence or perhaps by the course it did not take, but talked about, i.e. internalised violence and group suicide) was – like Armageddon itself – at hand. As this chapter has showed, Aum did not just talk about such matters: it took active steps to arm itself and to confront society. Clearly, as the sequence of events and pronouncements outlined in these chapters shows, Aum was, by 1994 – with its establishment of 'government' to defend it against the outside world – on a 'war footing': its leaders had convinced themselves that they had to fight their oppressors before they were themselves killed. They were, indeed, enveloped in a persecution complex in which death, destruction and salvation were interwoven, and which drew the movement into the sequence of events from 1993 onwards, when Aum clearly began to prepare for the conflict it felt was inevitable, to the sarin attacks of 1994 and 1995, which in themselves may have been conditioned by the need felt by Asahara and his followers to head off events.

Conclusions

In the preceding chapters I have attempted to highlight the factors and elements that conditioned Aum's path to violence, by outlining Aum's development from its origins as a yoga and meditation-centred movement of the 1980s, to the closed and highly structured movement of the 1990s, which believed that a cataclysmic war was at hand, inevitable and, indeed, essential. While I have suggested that the violent incidents it was responsible for were more likely to have been one-off responses to specific situations (the Matsumoto attack to head off a feared court judgment, the Tokyo attack to possibly respond to or pre-empt a raid, the Sakamoto murders to stop the lawyer from further embarrassing Aum with his investigations), it is clear, from the preparations Aum had made, that it intended to commit further and greater attacks.

In tracing Aum's path to violence I have emphasised a number of factors which contributed to this process. In particular I have drawn attention to Aum's basic stance as a world-rejecting religion, i.e. a religious movement that strongly criticised the mores of contemporary society and sought truth in the creation of an alternative, ideal(ised) society. This led Aum to an apo-calyptic vision in which it looked forward to the time when the corrupt world of the present would be rightfully destroyed and when a utopia would emerge. It also led Aum to establish a system of renunciates and communes, processes that inevitably drew the movement into conflict with mainstream society, and caused Aum to feel it was being oppressed, rejected and betrayed by society at large. This sense of betrayal was produced through the apparent rejection of Aum by the wider world on a number of levels (the lack of sufficient renunciates and people joining Aum, the sense of failure in its mission that this engendered, the humiliating rejection at the polls), and by conspiracies and attacks directed against Aum, in its view, by agents of a hostile and corrupt world, such as lawyers, parents and the media. The external conflicts Aum became involved in served to enhance the power and authority of the leadership – an authority that was unchallenged because of the hierarchic structures and the increasingly isolated, communal nature of the movement. These conflicts with the outside world, whether over land issues, residential registrations, or media investigations, all added to Aum's feeling (which was implicit in its world-rejectionist stance) that the outside world was corrupt, blind and headed to disasters of its own making.

This mixture of isolation and conflict fuelled the conspiracy theories that became increasingly important in Aum, and created the atmosphere in which what would otherwise appear to be rather ludicrous notions – that the US Airforce was showering poison gases on a small, obscure religious movement, that the media-popular wife of the Crown Prince was an active agent in a conspiracy to destroy Japan – could be accepted by Aum members as realities. By 1994 those fears and paranoias had escalated to the level that Aum could announce the formation of an alternative government, state that it needed to take measures to defend itself against the Japanese government, and even talk of the importance of striking at the wider society before it struck Aum, without seeming to cause consternation and open dissent among its followers.

Aum's development of a persecution complex in which it envisaged conspiracies wherever it looked, should also be seen as a manifestation of an Aum characteristic highlighted throughout this report, its inability to relate in a pragmatic or realistic way to the outside world. Aum consistently misjudged or misread the dynamics of the society in which it grew. The decision to build communes in conservative, rural areas is but one example of this lack of realism, for it placed the movement in precisely the sort of environment where it was most likely to encounter conflicts and strife. Its dealings with the media – which traditionally, in Japan, have been hostile to new religions – were shot through with this lack of realism. Aum sought to get attention through demonstrations of asceticism and claims about its leader's powers, but seems to have been ill-prepared to deal with the negative aspects of publicity which it was bound to attract by

putting itself so much in the public eye and by pursuing policies
that conflicted with standard Japanese social mores. It should also
have seen that claims such as those made over Asahara's DNA,
especially in the light of the complaints made against it, would be
examined by someone and found to be wanting, yet Aum seems
to have been unprepared for such an event. The decision to put up
candidates for election, coming so soon after the Sakamoto affair
and especially when combined with the manner in which Aum
ran its campaign, also suggests a movement estranged from
everyday realities. Surely, one has to ask, did Aum not realise that
its song, dance and elephant mask campaign was more likely to
attract derision than to bring success at the polls?

Another crucial issue was the way in which Asahara
appeared to raise the stakes concerning his own prophecies and,
hence, his credibility. When prophecies fail leaders need to
provide rationalisations of such failures, and these will be crucial
in determining whether the movement will subsequently be
saved or destroyed: if successful, as Trompf has put it, the
'members may then still look to the Millennium, but avoid the
mistake of proposing a time-table.'[1] Asahara made the mistake of
not only proposing a time-table, but of continually shortening the
time-scale in which the cataclysm was to occur. In his allegations
and prophecies from 1993 onwards Asahara gave himself and his
movement a very short time period for success or failure of his
message; he also allowed no space for any form of compromise.
Unlike the forms of millennialism espoused by many other
Japanese new religions, such as Agonshū, which says that through
its spiritual action the world will be saved (a way that leaves the
door open for Agonshū to claim, once 1999 has come and gone,
that it has in fact saved the world through its spiritual
endeavours), Aum set itself a decidedly more difficult task.
Claiming that destruction is inevitable and that only a few will
survive is actually a way of painting oneself into a very tight
corner: ironically, it is easier to 'save' all of humanity than just a
select few. To save all requires doing nothing; to save only a few
necessitates a real disaster that wipes out the bulk of humanity.

It is true that the dramatic proximity of Armageddon (first
prophesied as such in 1993, with, in 1995, prophecies that that
very year would see the beginnings of clear signals of its coming)

---

1.   Trompf 1990: 10.

encouraged many Aum waverers (admittedly pushed also, it appears, by internal strong-arm tactics) into becoming *shukkesha* and donating large sums to the movement. However, while such increasingly precarious prophecies worked internally as a strategy for increasing the commitment of some people who were already members, and for legitimating an increase in devotion to Asahara and an increase in the harshness of Aum's internal regime, it brought disaster in external terms. It locked the religion into a scenario from which it had little way out unless something drastic happened in the period leading up to 1997, and specifically in 1995, which Asahara had marked out as the year when the slide to destruction would begin. Quite simply, once the prophecies had been made, and their truth proclaimed, once Armageddon had been seen coming *without fail*, and once Asahara had made it clear not just that the cataclysm could not be prevented, but that in fact it was a necessary event to rid the world of its evils and to allow a true and ideal new world to emerge, then it had to occur for Asahara's and Aum's sakes. The failure of prophecies would undermine his status as a seer and would raise questions about the spiritual powers he claimed to have, and upon which Aum's hierarchy of attainment and initiation were built. The cataclysm prophesied thus had to occur, or if not, then at least some some fairly dramatic events had to happen to show that what he had been saying was on target, to reinforce his authority as a spiritual leader, and to verify the attainment of his disciples.

Asahara's prophesied millennium, and Aum's part in it, was of a dynamic rather than a passive type: by this I mean that he and his followers were not preparing to sit somewhere quietly and await the foretold millennium. Rather, they saw themselves as playing an active role in events. They had to prepare to defend themselves and make sure they survived. They were thus committed to action in the pursuit and attainment of the millennium. Thus the inevitability, indeed, the desirability, of destruction as a means to the attainment of Aum's religious goal, and the need for the fulfilment of Asahara's prophecies, fused with Aum's rising sense of persecution, whose origins derive from its very nature as a religion opposed to the ways of the ordinary world and to mainstream society, to put Aum on a 'war footing' with Japanese society, with disastrous repercussions not only for those killed or injured through its activities, but for the movement itself.

In the months after the subway attack, there have been numerous suggestions and assertions, particularly in the Japanese media, that Aum was not an 'authentic' religion but something else, an aberration from society or a military movement led by the demonic and power-mad Matsumoto/Asahara, which had assumed a religious guise as a means of carrying out its schemes.[2] I would argue that, based on the materials presented in this report, this proposition is not correct. The idea that, because it committed violence and engaged in military-style activities, Aum could not be a true or authentic religion implies, for a start, that 'true' religions do not commit acts of violence, which is a notion that simply does not stand up to scrutiny.

In fact, many of the factors contributing to the violence came about as they did because of Aum's religious characteristics. Its millennialist views, its focus on ascetic practices, the importance placed on initiation rituals, on prophecy, and on the power of a guru-figure who could provide these services, the drive amongst its members for higher levels of consciousness and for the transcendence of the ordinary human physical condition, and the focus on giving up worldly belongings in the hope of spiritual development, are all profoundly religious characteristics. So, too, is the world-rejection upon which Aum's original message was founded, and which eventually provided the impulses that led it to set itself apart from and in antithesis to society. So also, indeed, is the concept of persecution, which plays a dynamic and often empowering role in many religious movements, and which certainly played a large part in framing Aum's thinking in the 1990s. All these elements were important in shaping the way Aum acted and in taking it along the road it travelled.

As we have seen, it may well have been the emphasis placed on spiritual devotions and ascetic practices that planted the first seeds of violence in the movement. Asahara himself was involved in serious religious practices and austerities (he, for example, did the Agonshū *senza gyō* or 1000-day austerity, and practised yoga and meditation) and was convinced that austerities of a quite

---

2.   Shimosato 1995:253 suggests, for example, that Aum is not really a 'religion', whilst Kitabatake 1995 discusses Aum as an aberration and also argues that it should not be seen as a real religion. Such viewpoints have been expressed frequently in the numerous magazine and newspaper articles that have come out since March 1995, and have formed part of the rhetoric behind the process of disbanding Aum.

severe nature were extremely important in the development of spiritual consiousness, as was his insistence on the importance of initiation as a religious action. That Aum's members engaged in them with zeal and that they expressed their views that they were beneficial for them, is quite clear. Asahara's coercion of his wife, making her undergo such austerities, although she was reluctant, suggests that he really felt that they were crucial for her spiritual development, and that he placed enormous, and perhaps excessive, emphasis on their value. Whether it was because Asahara and his followers were insufficiently trained in the techniques of asceticism to see the potential dangers that it held, is unsure. What is certain, however, is that such zealous devotion to asceticism caused things to go wrong and allowed coercion and violence to be manifested inside the movement.

A recurrent element in discussions of the affair has, of course, been the position and personality of Asahara himself. In the confessions and reports of the trials that have so far emerged, it has become something of a repetitive theme amongst the accused that they were ordered to commit the crimes by Asahara, and that they were so under his spell that they could not refuse.[3] As mentioned in Chapter 1, Asahara has been demonised in the coverage of the affair as the evil influence who controlled the minds of his acolytes and manipulated them into committing crimes. Even the Japanese legal authorities appear to have been influenced by this line of thought, judging from their decision to try him separately because of fears that he would unduly influence his fellow defendants by his presence in court. Asahara's response, according to some news reports, has been to accept responsibility, as leader of the movement, for what the religion had done, but also to deny any direct blame for what happened. He has asked his prosecutors how a blind man such as he could do what he has been accused of, and has suggested that his aides were responsible: his blindness meant they could keep him in the dark about their schemes and plans.

3. Hayakawa, who has normally been seen as the No. 2 person in Aum, and who in the testimony of some of the accused has been alleged to have played a key role in the affair, has stated that he acted under Asahara's orders and that he was unaware of how the sarin he helped produce would be used (Asahi News Internet Service, Dec. 13 1995). Nakagawa Tomomasa, in admitting being involved in the Matsumoto case, has also given similar testimony, saying he was following 'orders and directions' (Asahi News Internet Service, January 1996).

The responses of Asahara and his aides are doubtless highly pragmatic. Since the death penalty, or at the very least extremely long prison sentences, await those found guilty and held responsible for the crimes, all the defendants have a vested interest in putting the blame on someone else.[4] This factor above all else is liable to make it difficult for any balanced assessment of the internal dynamics of the movement. I would, however, venture a number of comments on this issue. The first is that, although this report has largely, in terms of Aum personnel, focused on Asahara, this is because of his importance as the symbol of the movement and as the source of its legitimations and teachings. As leader of the movement he has to take ultimate responsibility for the actions of the organisation he created and led. However, this does not mean that he alone can be held responsible: he could not, of course, have carried out all of Aum's schemes without very close and active support from others in the movement. At the very least those around Asahara played a role in making him into the powerful figure he became in the movement. They helped create the aura that made him so powerful that members wanted to drink his bathwater and blood, and were prepared to pay for it: they in a real way helped to create the charismatic aura that surrounded him.

Indeed, many of his senior disciples played a major role in articulating messages similar to Asahara's: Hayakawa, for example, had published a book articulating Aum's view of Armageddon, looking forward to utopia and welcoming the catastrophe that would be required to bring it about.[5] Other leading members of Aum were active in giving public lectures and in publishing and contributing to books setting out Aum's teaching from early in the movement's history.[6] Many of Asahara's close followers were also better educated than he was: he had failed to get into the two universites (Kumamoto and Tokyo) for which he sat entrance

---

4.   The other person, besides Asahara, upon whom much of the blame is being cast by those who have been arraigned, is Murai Hideo. Murai was of course deeply involved as head of the agency that made sarin, but since he is dead, and cannot defend himself, he is a convenient scapegoat for all concerned, blamed by everyone as having played a leading part in the affair. He comes out, along with Asahara, as the major villian in the prosecution case in the Takahashi trial (see above, Chapter 4).

5.   *Shūkan Asahi* 1995 5/5.12, p. 25.

6.   See, for example, Aum Henshūbu (ed.) 1989, which consists of talks and writings by several of the religion's leading members, and Asahara (1995), which includes various talks and discussions by Asahara's chief disciples.

examinations, while many of those around had graduated from leading universities. Murai was a graduate of Osaka University, Hayakawa had a Masters degree in architecture from Osaka Prefectural University, Jōyu Fumihiro had a Masters degree in artificial intelligence from Waseda University and had worked briefly for the National Space Agency, and Tsuchiya had a Masters in organic chemistry from Tsukuba University. Thus it is possible that the other senior figures in the Aum hierarchy could have been as effective in determining what course Aum took as Asahara was, or even that they could have influenced or even manipulated him. I stress that I am not arguing that this was the case, or seeking to diminish Asahara's guilt: rather, I am putting these points forward as possible issues to consider in further discussions of the case.

Comparative Perspectives: Two Windows on the Aum Affair

Asahara's point about his blindness is relevant. He is not accused of actually having placed the sarin on the subway trains or of having personally released sarin in Matsumoto or of making the poison gas himself. His followers did all of these things. No doubt these were done under his orders, but the question at the heart of this matter is why did his followers carry out his orders with such zeal? One of the crucial questions that comes up in the Aum affair is why there appears to have been little protest in the religion as it moved from idealism to confrontation, and why the members of Aum appeared to have gone along with the thinking processes that, especially after 1989, created the atmosphere of growing violence around the movement. To gain some insights into how this process could have happened in Aum, and also to place the affair in a wider perspective, I shall here draw some parallels with two other cases in which movements with a closed structure (i.e. they drew clear boundaries between themselves and the wider world) manifested signs of violence and hostility. One of these cases, which involves the violent implosion of the Japanese left-wing terrorist movement the Rengō Sekigun in 1972,[7] provides us with an example of how Japanese social

---

7.   Comparisons with the Rengō Sekigun affair have been made by a number of Japanese commentators in recent months, although these have usually been framed within the types of interpretation mentioned above, in which Aum is portrayed as really a military organisation rather than a religious one. Shimosato 1995: 254, for example, makes the comparison with Rengō Sekigun, but with an emphasis on 'military' questions. As indicated here, in my view the important point of comparison is in terms of what the affair says about Japanese social dynamics and about issues of cognitive dissonance.

dynamics within a closed group might contribute to, rather than act as a barrier to, the development of violence. The other case to be discussed is that of the Rajneesh movement and centres on some of the incidents that occurred at and around the commune of this movement in rural Oregon in the USA in the 1980s. The Rajneesh case, besides displaying some rather striking similarities with the Aum affair, affords us further insights into what went on in Aum, from a comparative religious perspective.

Patricia G. Steinhoff, in her valuable essay on the destructive internal purge in the Japanese Red Army faction Rengō Sekigun, that took place in the mountains of Nagano prefecture in 1972 leading to the deaths of 12 of its members, has drawn attention to the question of cognitive dissonance, of the ways in which followers, especially of small groups, will reinterpret external realities to make them fit with the internal logic and ideology of their movement. What concerns Steinhoff are the social dynamics that caused the purge, in which members of what was originally a small group of dedicated extreme left-wing militants and comrades, while seeking to purify their revolutionary thoughts, participated in a distructive purge inside their own group. To Steinhoff the real horror of the purge was that it was carried out by what she sees as quite normal people and resulted from ordinary social processes.[8] In looking at the command structures of this movement, she notes (following Weber) that

> the central question about authority is why people acquiesce to it. It is not sufficient to understand how Mori [author's note: the leader of Rengō Sekigun] led; one must also explain why others followed more or less willingly.[9]

Steinhoff suggests a number of factors that caused the members to go along with their leader: the followers had lost their confidence in their own ability to judge matters; expressing reservations about the course of events (as people were being killed inside the faction) became dangerous; expressions of doubt were seized on as manifestations of weaknesss that rendered the person liable to attack; and the Japanese group process is not conducive to direct expression of opposition to leaders or to the group as a whole.[10] Once a group has decided to accept a

---

8. Steinhoff 1992: 195.
9. Ibid. p. 212.
10. Ibid. p. 212

leader's authority, there are no real mechanisms for checking or providing an alternative to the leader's interpretation of events, for that would appear to be challenging an accepted consensus. Members are thus carried along with the tide of group dynamics, in which once the leader has been accepted as such, followers find it extremely difficult to oppose his voice, even if his behaviour becomes erratic and unpredictable. Equally, once a course of action has been set in motion, through such group dynamic processes, members feel obliged to support it because of consensual obligations.

What happened in Rengō Sekigun was that the methods the leader Mori developed in order to purify the revolutionary spirit of the group members, and to discipline members who had manifested their lack of such purity, led to an escalation of physical force and punishments being used against group members. When a member of the group died, unexpectedly, as a result of these punishments, in which all other group members had participated, there was a potential opportunity for the group to have pulled back from further violence. However, Mori produced an explanation of why this unexpected death had happened that managed to absolve himself and the others from blame. His interpretation was that the man concerned, Ozaki, had died of defeatism: he had been unable to achieve the levels of revolutionary purity sought by the group, and had thus died of shock. No matter how problematic such an explanation might appear from an external perspective, in the situation at hand this explanation had a logic of its own. It exonerated the participants in the beatings of having murdered Ozaki, and showed that he

> had *chosen* defeat and death because he had not been strong enough to achieve the state of communist transformation, despite their help.[11]

The victim, rather than the perpetrators, was thus blamed for his death. In the group dynamics in which members of the revolutionary group had accepted Mori as the leader and had acquiesced in the actions he had originally set in motion (i.e. punishing those who were deemed to have displayed revolutionary shortcomings) this view came to represent the reality of the situation and members began to reinterpret the new realities within the ideological framework into which they were locked.

11. Ibid. p. 208.

As Steinhoff notes, by accepting the death-by-defeatism interpretation, they accepted advance responsibility for their own deaths through similar means: the only way to avoid such a fate was to overcome defeatism and be more zealous.[12] The group members had thus lost confidence in their own abilities to judge the situation, and increasingly relied on their leader's explanations which helped them create a new logic for their situation and which exonerated them from blame in the death of a colleague. At the same time the escalating fears they felt as their fellow members were in turn set upon and purged for their failings, stopped them from protesting. Protest would, in itself, have been an expression of weakness and of lack of revolutionary zeal, and would thus have been an expression of defeatism, which could be a fatal condition. The closed, and isolated, nature of the group (they were on the run from the police and holed up in cabins in the mountains of central Japan) was a vital factor in the process:

> The Rengō Sekigun purge gained much of its momentum because it occurred in a closed system, a total situation in which participants fed on their own rhetoric and emotions without any external reality to serve as a corrective. [13]

We can see many parallels with Aum in this incident. Members who had already yielded up their worldly status and wealth, and had committed themselves (for reasons connected with a desire to attain enlightenment or spiritual fulfilment) to Aum's communes, command structures and initiatory hierarchies, were left with little choice but to follow the shifts and changes within the movement. Asahara's increasingly paranoid talk of external threats became, for such people, a reality that, because they had abandoned their own confidence in making judgements, they were increasingly unable to question. As Noda Naruhito has stated in an interview, while he did not absolutely believe Asahara's claims that Aum was under attack, at that time (i.e. around 1994) there was such a 'persecution complex' surrounding Aum that members could readily accept such negative views of the outside world and go along with them.[14] Voicing dissent became an impossibility, too, not only in the light of the

---

12. Ibid. p. 209.
13. Ibid. p. 216
14. *Shūkan Asahi* Oct. 13th 1995, pp. 25-26.

Taguchi case but also in the environment of persecution and external threat that Aum built around itself.

When things began to go wrong, the explanations given by Asahara to his followers – that there was a conspiracy against Aum and that the outside world was hostile and rotten – had an appealing logic to the movement's members who had, it is important to remember, joined Aum and its communes precisely because they wished to renounce that society. The continuing explanations of the evils of society, of the lack of merit of those in it, and of the conspiracies they were mounting against Aum, all served to transfer whatever blame there might be in terms of Aum's acts of violence away from the perpetrators and towards the victims, who had chosen to live in the corrupt material world that was about to be destroyed. Hence they had effectively chosen death over the utopian and enlightened life offered them by Aum.

The hierarchy and adherence to cultural norms that played a part in the Rengō Sekigun affair and that meant there were few if any barriers that could halt the process once violence had begun, or that could rein in a leader once the group had accepted him as such, operated also in the Aum case. Aum members, like those of Rengō Sekigun, thus not only went along with their leaders but also interpreted events within the framework of their movement's internal ideology and logic. Thus Aum's closed, communal and hierarchic structure, and its increasing focus on an explosive, conspiracy-bound rhetoric infused with predictions of violence (either of the end of the world or of violence against Aum) produced the momentum towards violence while providing internal rationalisations of this process.

The Rengō Sekigun provides us with an example of the processes of cognitive dissonance in action, and of the means of understanding aspects of the Aum affair through the lens of Japanese social dynamics. Similar questions concerned with cognitive dissonance are also present in another affair which is worth examining in connection with Aum, since it displays many fascinating parallels with this case, and since it provides us with an example, from outside Japan, of a religion that became embroiled in both internal and external violence, as well as conflict with a surrounding community. This is the case of the Rajneesh movement and the problems that developed around the commune it built in rural Oregon in the USA.

The Rajneesh movement was founded in India by the Indian religious leader, Bhagwan Shree Rajneesh. It was, like Aum, extremely eclectic and used a variety of religious techniques in the pursuit of religious liberation. It appealed to many highly educated and well-qualified Westerners who travelled to India to visit their guru's ashram at Poona. The movement, however, encountered much local hostility due to the lifestyle of its members and because of the techniques and teachings of Rajneesh; there are also suggestions, according to Gordon, that Rajneesh and his leading followers deliberately provoked matters in order to create tensions in Poona and thus legitimate a move to the USA to establish a township on land that the movement had purchased at Antelope in Oregon.[15]

The move to Oregon was done with little consultation with the movement's followers, and was one in a number of rapid shifts and changes in Rajneesh's teachings and actions, which were often imposed on the followers without warning. Rajneesh himself became increasingly unpredictable, acting strangely, making frequent allegations against his followers or the outside world and complaining of illness and the like, so that his followers were constantly kept guessing as to what would come next. As Gordon has shown in his study of Rajneesh, his followers, who had committed themselves to his commune, often making large financial commitments in the process, reacted to his behaviour first with bewilderment, and then moved to rationalisations, explanations and understandings. The ways in which followers explained or legitimated his collecting of Rolls Royces and other such extravagances and oddities, and the ways in which they rationalised later odd developments such as his dramatic attempt to escape from Oregon and leave the USA at a time when he came under police investigation for criminal activities, show a mixture of faith and bewilderment, a wish to follow the guru, and a commitment to him which allowed them to argue that there must be some ulterior, spiritual reason behind his actions. As Gordon shows, members were capable of formulating numerous rationalisations to explain his actions and absolve him of censure, often stating, as they did, that through his actions 'Bhagwan was testing us', an explanation often cited, for example, with regard to his apparent love of material goods and his collection of Rolls

---

15. Gordon 1987: 94-95.

Royces in which he drove around the commune. Everything became, in their eyes,

> a device to increase awareness, to deepen surrender, and their connection to their Master.[16]

Rajneesh's followers also endured immense pressure to give large sums of money, especially to develop the movement's ambitions to build the city of Rajneeshpuram on the land it had acquired in Oregon. These pressures often carried underlying threats attached: donations moved from being demonstrations of one's lack of attachment to material things, to being expressions of (and evidence of) one's commitment and devotion to the guru. The urgency of collecting money appears also to have infected Rajneesh: the building of Rajneeshpuram required huge sums, and the apparent frailty of Rajneesh's health made it essential that all this was done as fast as possible. Rajneesh's illnesses increased his remoteness from his disciples and heightened his authority, causing his disciples to regard him with increasing warmth (because, as they were told, he might not be with them for long) and to limit any critical feedback about him amongst his followers.[17]

The financial manipulation of the followers was also linked to his increasing remoteness from them: Rajneesh in Oregon was surrounded by, or surrounded himself with, a small inner group of close disciples, who controlled access to him and created an increasing aura of charisma around him. Remoteness serves to encourage a sense of awe, while closeness, easy access and familiarity tend to decrease such sentiments, a point Rajneesh's entourage understood well. Thus, citing his illnesses and allergies as reasons why access to him had to be limited, they helped to increase his stature by decreasing his contact with his followers. As the movement grew and developed more formal organisational and bureaucratic structures, access became even more difficult and controlled, so that even those who had moved to Rajneeshpuram could not get ready access to him.

The movement quickly ran into conflicts with its neighbours. The conservative local farming community was worried that the Rajneesh community would outnumber and outvote them, thereby taking over the local council: they were thus hostile to the

---

16. Ibid. p. 81.
17. Ibid. pp. 116-117.

community from the beginning, a hostility fuelled also by the fact that the Rajneesh movement's social and sexual attitudes differed immensely from their own. The fears of the local community were realised in many ways: the Rajneesh commune attempted to wrest control of the region through manipulating the electoral process, and on numerous occasions it rode roughshod over local sentiments and regulations in developing its plans. While recognising that the local community, due to its often hostile and prejudiced attitudes, shared in the blame for the conflicts that developed, James Gordon (himself in many ways a Rajneesh sympathiser) noted how the Rajneesh commune members behaved with 'arrogance and obtuseness' towards the Oregon locals, and displayed an 'easy contempt for outsiders – their intelligence as well as their laws.'[18]

Tensions gradually grew around the commune, and an atmosphere developed in which exploitative, coercive and hostile behaviour became an accepted norm within the movement and in its relationships to the external world. Commune members were regarded as potential traitors and subjected to intimidation,[19] and members were ordered to break off contact with anyone who did leave. As some people did leave, there were growing fears that the commune might collapse, and this caused an escalation of violence and intimidation inside the movement in order to strengthen loyalty.[20] Apocalyptic visions began to find their way into Rajneesh's teaching: Nostradamus was invoked to demonstrate that time was running out, and predictions were made that a nuclear holocaust or some other disaster (in which the AIDS virus figured prominently) would wipe out the world and to illustrate the urgency of building a utopia as soon as possible. As Gordon notes, in terms which are remarkably similar to those I have described in the Aum case, 'Rajneesh infused his utopian project with an apocalyptic urgency'.[21] As these ideas of the urgency of building utopia now, and of averting the apocalypse,

---

18. Ibid. p. 105.

19. Ibid. p. 134.

20. Parallels can also be drawn, in terms of the issue of loyalty, with the Jonestown suicides: as Maaga shows, it was when leading members began to defect that the Jonestown community faced the possibility of collapse, and, in her analysis, chose the option of remaining together through suicide rather than risking fragmentation through defections (Maaga 1995).

21. Ibid. p. 131, and pp. 236-237.

developed in Rajneesh's movement, so too did the fears of conspiracies against it, orchestrated by the US government.[22] There were even fears raised about the purpose of flights over the commune by Navy aircraft from a nearby base, which appeared to be part of this conspiracy against the movement,[23] and accusations that external enemies were conspiring to attack and kill Rajneesh.[24]

The 'response' of Rajneesh's inner circle was to develop plans to strike at their enemies and 'oppressors' outside. The leaders collected arms to defend the commune against the perceived threats from outside,[25] and later formulated plans to deal with their external enemies through the use of poison. A secret laboratory was built where attempts to produce poisons and toxic bacteria were carried out, plans were drawn up to isolate the AIDS virus and spread it among the local community, and a 'hit-list' of targets for assassination was drawn up, including the State Attorney-General and several other leading legal figures in the region.[26] Eventually the community at Rajneeshpuram was rent asunder by allegations of violence in- and outside the commune. Rajneesh fled (he was arrested by the American authorities but allowed to leave the country after pleading guilty to a minor charge relating to immigration fraud, and was not allowed back again), while several of his leading supporters were arraigned on charges ranging from financial crimes to attempts to poison members of the surrounding community. Some were also charged with, and eventually found guilty of, charges of conspiring to kill members of the state's law enforcement bodies, and several were sentenced to periods of imprisonment.[27] In the aftermath of the affair many of Rajneesh's followers remained prepared to exonerate him from guilt in the affair, which was seen as having been perpetrated by a small group of leading acolytes who had seized control of the commune and kept him in the dark as to what was happening. Rajneesh himself blamed these followers, particularly his chief aide, Ma Anand Sheela (who

22. Ibid. p. 164.
23. Ibid. p. 137.
24. Ibid. p. 183.
25. Ibid. p. 134.
26. Ibid. pp. 182-183.
27. Ibid. pp. 207-208.

pleaded guilty to the charges against her and was sent to prison), for all the problems that had occurred.[28]

The Rajneesh affair thus presents us with some parallels to the Aum case, not just in terms of the processes whereby followers accepted and rationalised the behaviour and pronouncements of their leader, but also in the course of events that occurred. The patterns of internal violence, the apocalyptic visions, the urgency these created in the community, the conspiracies against the movement and its responses, including the secret development of poisons, are remarkably similar to what went on, albeit in a more destructive way, in Aum. There are also parallels between the ways in which the Rajneesh commune developed, conflicted with the local community, and produced an increasingly closed system of authority, and the events at Kamikuishiki, and in the ways that the movements began to demand commitments in financial terms from their followers.

Gordon suggests that Rajneesh and his followers came increasingly to see the world in black and white terms, in which the people inside the commune were righteous: they were a chosen people who were going to save the world, while the outside world was dangerous, dying and condemned. As this perception of things took place, Rajneesh and his immediate advisers became increasingly dictatorial, and turned the commune – their utopia – into something approaching a concentration camp.[29]

In particular, too, the Rajneesh case suggests that it is where the leader/guru figure is surrounded by a coterie of powerful followers, who control access to him and build up his charisma, that dangers occur and that the excesses of power can develop. In the Rajneesh case he was able to avoid going to court on the most serious charges and to pass the blame onto those around him. However, as Gordon shows in his conclusion, neither he nor his advisers could have acted alone: the events at Rajneeshpuram were the product also of the interactions between him and his followers. Although it may be many years before any sober testimony will become available of how the leaders of Aum Shinrikyō interacted as they did, I suspect that evidence of something similar will also emerge here that will provide us with a deeper understanding of the events that evolved betwen 1989

---

28. Ibid. p. 190.
29. Ibid. pp. 236-237.

and 1995. Although Asahara Shōkō, as the leader and source of inspiration of Aum Shinrikyō, was at the heart of the Aum affair, he was surrounded by others who reinforced his own aspirations and paranoias, allowed them to go unchecked and went along with his orders to create mass destruction. In that compliance and acquiescence one can see possible parallels with the events at Rajneeshpuram. It is also the hidden and, currently, the least known part of the whole cocktail of factors which led Aum to violence, but it is an area that requires further research, and perhaps further comparative study.

The Rengō Sekigun affair shows us how, within the context of Japanese social settings, especially in the pressurised atmosphere of a closed group, the types of social dynamics which lead a group to take part in, accept and rationalise violence, can develop. The Rajneesh case also shows us how, in a different country and situation, violence and hostility can emerge from within a closed religious community that stands in opposition to the world around it. These cases do not, I must stress, mean that violence is bound to occur in all closed religious groups or all tightly-knit Japanese social organisations in conflict with the society around them. However, they do show us that what went on in and around Aum was not unique, but manifested certain patterns and reflected certain social dynamics and religious models that have occurred before. The crucial issue is why some religions, even idealistic ones that preach the virtues of renunciation and meditation, find themselves on a path that leads them to violence. It is this issue that this study, in describing the issues and events surrounding Aum Shinrikyō in its development from the 1980s to 1995, has sought to discuss.

The Aum Affair: Public Reactions and Repercussions

Although this study has concentrated on the evolution of the Aum affair up to March 1995, it is apposite to make a few comments about its effects, so far, in Japan and on some of the issues that are going to be central to subsequent discussions of the affair.

For much of 1995 after March the affair dominated the Japanese media and the nation: it was the lead item in the news for weeks at a time, with most newspapers and magazines devoting large amounts of space to it, while television coverage was even greater, with some stations virtually ran Aum-related programmes all day, for weeks on end. An 'Aum industry' developed, with media pundits and 'experts' analysing and commenting on events and developments, and seeking to find messages, meanings and morals in the affair for Japanese society. Coming at a time when Japan was in the midst of the deepest economic recession in the post-war era, and still suffering in the aftermath of the Hanshin earthquake, the biggest single natural catastrophe in Japan for over 70 years, the sarin attack on crowded commuter trains at rush-hour intensified the public mood of unease, shattering, for many people, the widely held image of public safety in Japan. The continuing media revelations in the affair heightened this sense of unease, and called into question, for many people, the competence of the public authorities. In particular questions were asked of the police: why had they apparently failed to be aware of Aum's activities and to investigate earlier incidents, such as the Sakamoto case, properly? How was a small religious movement able to stockpile weapons and materials that could be used for offensive purposes, without anyone apparently being aware of this?

The affair has added fresh life to numerous ongoing debates about the nature and direction of Japanese society and education, and has contributed to a fresh bout of the intensive navel gazing that the Japanese are fond of. Discussions asking what the affair says about the nature of Japanese society in general have been a prominent feature of this particular response to the affair, with questions being raised about why so many young and highly educated people found it so abhorrent that they wanted to cut themselves off from this society in a communal and world-rejecting movement, and ultimately wanted to destroy it altogther.

Questions have also been raised about the role of the media in the affair, partly because of the voyeuristic way in which the affair has been presented, and because of the endless recycling of rumours, which have clouded some of the issues and which have often been reported as 'facts' in the affair. There have been criticisms, also, that the media in general were more concerned with sensationalising the case and with treating it as a spectacle than in actually reporting it accurately, a criticism that became especially strong after the murder of Murai Hideo, which occurred in front of television cameras which continued to record the incident (cf. Indroduction). The murder was subsequently broadcast repeatedly in Japan by many television stations, leading to some public anger at the media, who were criticised for this apparent disregard of basic standards of decency.[30]

Academics, also, have come under fire in the affair. Questions have been raised about why no-one in the academic community sems to have been aware of the dangers posed by Aum. This question has been relatively easily answered, in that there are many new religions in Japan, but far fewer scholars who study them: hence it is likely at any one time for there to be numerous active movements about whom relatively little is known. In the Aum case, however, the issue was complicated by the fact that two scholars, Shimada Hiromi and Nakazawa Shin'ichi, had both visited Aum premises, met and been photographed with Asahara on occasion. They had both included favourable comments on the movement (particularly in connection to the apparent dedication of Aum members to their ascetic practices) in materials they had published. Photographs of both academics alongside Asahara have been used in Aum publications to portray the movement in a good light and imply that it had received a seal of academic approval. Shimada, in particular, has come under fire because of these issues, and was subsequently suspended (and later dismissed) by his university on charges of bringing it into disrepute.[31]

The affair also appears to have undermined academic critiques of media and journalistic approaches to new and supposedly 'deviant' religious movements. Scholars have frequently criticised media discussions of new religions in particular because they appear to focus on the sensational, portraying them as deviant movements that threaten social stability and family values, usually focusing as they do on what are called 'atrocity stories' (i.e. reports of things going wrong or of people being badly treated by new religions).[32] This tendency has also been quite pronounced in Japan, where the media in

---

30. See the comments reported in Hardacre (1995: 21), in which members of the public reacted angrily to the endless showing of his death: he might have been, one person wrote to the *Asahi Shinbun*, a criminal, but to show his death in such a way violated human decency.

31. Mullins 1995: p. 10.

32. For general discussion of the questions of how new religions may be dealt with or misrepresented by the media see Richardson 1983, esp. pp. 101-104 , Beckford 1983, esp. pp. 56-61, and Barker 1984. On the issue of 'atrocity tales' see Shupe and Bromley 1981.

general (and the weekly magazines and some of the more conservative newspapers in particular) have appeared more interested in exposés of and attacks on new movements, than they have been on balanced representations of their views. In this case, played out as it was in the full glare of the media spotlight, the media's concerns with new religions as dangerous and deviant appeared to be legitimated: here was a religion that had committed atrocities, and that had become dangerous and subversive. The fact that the academics who had looked at Aum had given it an apparently clean bill of health, while some journalists had voiced opinions that it was potentially dangerous several years before 1995, has added strength to this argument.[33] The affair, as a result, has also had, and will continue to have, repercussions in the portrayal and study of religion in Japan.

The most critical debates, however, have centred around the constitutional protection of religion in Japan, and the effects that the affair has had, and will have, on the status of religion in Japan, and these in particular will continue to be important for some time to come. Coming so soon after the Hanshin earthquake, which itself led to many criticisms being levelled against mainstream religious groups that they were slow to respond or provide moral support or care for the victims,[34] the affair appeared to portray religion in a negative light. One scholar, Yamaori Tetsuo, even suggested that the affair sounded the death knell for religion in Japan for, he argued, not only had the earthquake shown the older religions to be inert and incapable of providing practial help in the face of crisis, but the Aum affair had appeared to validate the criticisms of rationalists and Marxist intellectuals that religion was pernicious, dangerous and ridden with superstitions and hence out of place in a modern society.[35] Religious organisations in general displayed a seeming inability to produce clear responses to the Aum affair, and have been criticised by concerned scholars as a result.[36] Rather than attempting to discuss the issues and develop a debate about the

---

33. Egawa Shōko in particular had been quite vocal in portraying Aum as a dangerous movement in the aftermath of the Sakamoto affair, and had been active in publishing criticisms of the movement (see Egawa 1995).

34. See, for example, Repp's article in *Japanese Religions* (1995), which makes some critical remarks about the ways some religious movements responded to this crisis.

35. Yamaori 1995.

36. See, for example, Kisala 1995 and Brennan 1995.

role of religion in Japanese contemporary society, most organisations seemed more intent on maintaining a low profile, acting
as if the affair was not really a matter of their concern, or merely
suggesting that it was a regrettable incident.

In the long-term, the most crucial repercussions of the affair
may be in the reforms of the Religious Corporations Law, which
are under discussion, and on the ways in which this will affect the
relationship between state and religion. The laws governing and
protecting religion in Japan were framed in the light of pre-war
state repressions of religious organisations, and with the
perspective that religions require protection from the state. For
those who have wished to alter this situation, the Aum affair has
suggested that the state also needs to be protected from religions,
and that some change in the law is thus required. Although, in the
light of the Aum affair, there may be widespread public support
for some curbs to be placed on religious movements, to scrutinise
their activities and, in particular, to impose some control on their
financial dealings and on the favourable tax concessions they
currently have, there have also been widesprerad concerns that
any attempt to impose state supervision on religions could have
widespread repercussions in the field of civil liberties and on the
freedom of religion in general. More pertinently, in the short term
at least, is the fact that the government's wish to rein in religious
movements by law is conditioned by the fact that the largest
religious organisation in Japan, the lay Buddhist organisation
Sōka Gakkai, is the main supporter of one of the largest political
groups in the Japanese political Opposition party Shinshintō, and
that it is able to mobilise a very large number of votes and
campaigners for the opposition in elections. Thus, underlying the
government's seeming wish to impose controls on religions in
order to protect state and society, is the clear ambition to restrict
and strike at one of its main political enemies.[37]

The Aum Affair in Retrospect

In the previous section I have attempted to briefly outline some
of the questions, issues and debates that have been thrown up in

---

37. The outline for a bill drafted by the Liberal Democratic Party (the main
plank in the government coalition) in January 1996 on religious corporations
would ban them from forming political parties and would further restrict
their activities – in other words, it seems designed to hit strongly at Sōka
Gakkai.

the aftermath of the affair and that will continue to be of concern for some time to come. In particular the issues surrounding the relationship between religion and state, and over possible reforms of the Religious Corporations Law, will be of central concern in the immediate future, and these will have immense repercussions on the Japanese political as well as religious worlds. At this stage, however, these are not areas and topics that can be fully discussed within the context of this report, although they are clearly matters that need to be taken into consideration in subsequent considerations of the affair. The purpose of this report has been to discuss the factors that led to the Aum affair and to illuminate some of the causes and issues in its devlopment. As these concluding comments have illustrated, however, the affair is not over yet; its repercussions will be felt in Japanese religious, social and political arenas for some time to come, and it and its aftermath will require continuing study by scholars for many years to come.

References

Asahara Shōkō, 1986. *Chōnōryoku: himitsu no kaihatsuhō* (Tokyo: Aum Shuppan).

——, 1989. *Metsubō no hi* (Tokyo: Aum Shuppan).

——, 1991. *Asahara Shōkō za samadi* [*The Samadhi*] (Tokyo: Aum Shuppan).

——, 1992. *Declaring Myself the Christ* (Tokyo: Aum Shuppan).

——, 1993. *Asahara Shōkō, senritsu no yogen* (Tokyo: Aum Shuppan).

——, 1995. *Hi izuru kuni, saiwaichikashi* (Tokyo: Aum Shuppan).

Asahara Shōkō, (ed.) 1992. *Risōshakai Shambala 9* (Tokyo: Aum Shuppan).

Astley, Trevor, 1995. 'The transformation of a recent Japanese new religion: Okawa Ryūhō and Kōfuku no Kagaku', *Japanese Journal of Religious Studies* 22: 3–4, pp. 343–380.

Aum Shinrikyō, (ed), n.d. *Shugyō* (Tokyo: Aum Shuppan).

Aum Translation Committee, (ed), 1992. *Your First Steps to Truth* (Fujinomiya: Aum Publishing).

Barker, Eileen, 1984. *The Making of a Moonie: Choice or Brainwashing?* (Oxford: Blackwells).

Beckford, James, 1983. 'The Public Response to New Religious Movements in Britain', *Social Compass* 30/1: 49–62.

Brennan, Noah S., 1995. 'A Religious Response to the Aum Affair', *Japan Quarterly* Oct–Dec 1995: 384–390.

Egawa Shōko, 1995. *Kyūseishu no yabō* (Tokyo: Kyōikushiryō Shuppankai).

Fujita Shōichi, 1995. *Aum Shinrikyō jiken* (Tokyo: Asahi News Shop).

Gordon, James S., 1987. *The Golden Guru* (Lexington, Va: Stephen Greene Press).

Hardacre, Helen, 1995. *Aum Shinrikyō and the Japanese media: The Pied Piper meets the Lamb of God* (Columbia University: East Asian Institute Report).

Inoue Nobutaka, Takeda Michio and Kitabatake Kiyoyasu, 1995. *Aum Shinrikyō to wa nanika* (Tokyo: Asahi News Shop).

Inoue Nobutaka et al., 1991. *Shin shūkyō jiten* (Tokyo: Kōbundō).

Kiriyama Seiyū, 1971. *Henshin no genri* (Tokyo: Kadokawa Bunko).

Kisala, Robert, 1995. 'Aum Alone in Japan: religious responses to the "Aum affair"', *Bulletin of the Nanzan Institute for Religion and Culture* 19: 6–34.

Kitabatake Kiyoyasu, 1995. 'Aum Shinrikyō: Society Begets an Aberration', *Japan Quarterly* Oct–Dec 1995: 376–383.

Kumamoto Nichinichi Shinbun, (ed), 1992. *Aum Shinrikyō to mura no ronri* (Fukuoka: Ashi Shobō).

Lifton, Robert Jay, 1961. *Thought Reform and the Psychology of Totalism* (New York: Norton).

Maaga, Mary, 1995. 'Loyalty and Freedom, a deadly potion: a consideration of the Jonestown suicides' (paper delivered at the AAR conference, Philadelphia Nov. 19, 1995).

Mainichi Shinbun Shūkyō Shuzaihan, (ed), 1993. *Kiseimatsu no kamisama* (Tokyo: Tōhō Shuppan).

Miyadai Shinji, 1995. 'Ryōshin no hanzaisha', *Takarashima* No. 30: 28–39.

Morioka Kiyomi, 1994. 'Attacks on the new religions: Risshō Kōseikai and the "Yomiuri affair"', *Japanese Journal of Religious Studies* 21: 2–3: 281–310.

Mullins, Mark, 1995. 'Aum Shinrikyō as an apocalyptic movement: a review of recent Japanese responses', (paper given at the SSSR conference, USA, Oct. 1995).

Numata Kenya, 1987. 'Gendai shinshūkyō ni okeru karisuma', In Shūkyō Shakai Gakken Kenkyūkai, (ed), *Kyōso to sono shūhen* (Tokyo: Yūzankaku): 70–90.

——, 1988. *Gendai Nihon no shinshūkyō* (Osaka: Sōgensha).

——, 1995. *Shūkyō to kagaku no neoparadimu: shinshin shūkyō o chūshintoshite* (Osaka: Sōgensha).

Reader, Ian, 1991.1988, 'The Rise of a Japanese "New New Religion": Themes in the Development of Agonshū', *Japanese Journal of Religious Studies* 15/4: 235-261.

——, *Religion in Contemporary Japan* (Honolulu: University of Hawaii).

——, 1994. 'Appropriated Images: esoteric themes in a Japanese new religion', In Ian Astley, (ed), *Esoteric Buddhism in Japan* (Copenhagen: Seminar for Buddhist Studies): 37–64.

Repp, Martin, 1995. 'The Earthquake in the Kobe-Osaka Area January 17th 1995: Its Impact on Religions and Their Response', *Japanese Religions* 20/2: 207–229.

Richardson, James T., 1983. 'New Religious Movements in the United States: a Review', *Social Compass* 30/1: 85–110.

Shimada, Hiromi, 1995. *Shinji yasui kokoro* (Tokyo: PHP).

Shimazono Susumu, 1992. *Shinshin shūkyō to shūkyō būmu* (Tokyo: Iwanami Booklets No.237).

——, 1995. *Aum Shinrokyō no kiseki* (Tokyo: Iwanami Booklets No. 379).

Shimosato Masaaki, 1995. *Akuma no shiroi kiri* (Tokyo: Pocket Books Ltd).

Shūkyō Hōjin Oumu Shinrikyō (March 1995 broadsheet), *Rachi shita no wa keisatsu!* (Osaka: Shūkyō Hōjin Oumu Shinrikyō).

Shupe, Anson D. and Bromley, David G., 1981. 'Apostates and Atrocity Stories: some parameters in the dynamics of deprogramming', in B. Wilson, (ed), *The Social Impact of New Religious Movements* (New York: Edwin Mellen Press) pp. 179–215.

Steinhoff, Patricia G., 1992. 'Defeat by defeatism and other fables: the social dynamics of the Rengō Sekigun purge', In Takie Sugiyama Lebra, (ed.), *Japanese Social Organizations* (Honolulu: University of Hawaii): 195–224.

Trompf, G. W., 1990. 'Introduction', In G.W. Trompf, (ed), *Cargo Cults and Millenarian Movements* (Berlin: Mouton de Gruyter): 1–32.

Yamaori Tetsuo, 1995. 'Aum jiken to Nihon shūkyō no shūen', *Shokun* 27/6: 34–47.

Young, Richard Fox, 1995. 'Lethal achievements: Fragments of a response to the Aum Shinrikyō affair', *Japanese Religions* Vol. 20: 2: 230–245.

The above material has been supplemented by Japanese news sources, both televison, magazines, newspapers, and on-line Internet services. The following newspapers and magazines have been either cited or used as sources:

Japanese-language newspapers

Asahi Shinbun

Mainichi Shinbun

Yomiuri Shinbun

English-language newspapers

Daily Yomiuri

Mainichi Daily News

Japan Times

Internet Service of the Asahi Shinbun

Japanese magazines

Aera

Shūkan Asahi

Sunday Mainichi

Shūkan Yomiuri

"Without doubt the scholar bests the journalists."
– Monumenta Nipponica

What the critics have been saying about **A Poisonous Cocktail**

Both the following reviews compare Ian Reader's study with three other early studies of the Aum affair, rating it head and shoulders above the others. Perhaps this is an unfair comparison as the other three works could be said to be instant books responding to the intense media coverage of the affair. Recently, however, an extensive Japanese-language study of the Aum affair by Shimazono Susumu was published. This praises and extensively cites from *A Poisonous Cocktail*, but it has not been possible to include these comments here.

∅

[This book] provides a valuable overview of Aum's history and in its involvement in the attack on the Tokyo subway system and other criminal acts of violence. Although Reader is one of the leading scholars of religion in contemporary Japan and thus was well positioned to undertake this study, it is still quite an achievement to turn out such a solid, well-documented study in such short order. His book is at least as good as the the few serious studies of Aum in Japanese that have been published in the past year and it will provide a starting point for future discussion, debate and study.

– Monumenta Nipponica (vol. 51, no. 3, 1996)

∅

Ian Reader's A Poisonous Cocktail offers the best early scholarly analysis of the Aum affair. ... His balanced presentation on Aum places the group within the context of New Religions and 'New Age' thought and activity in Japan. He provides a superb overview of Aum's history, leadership, ideology, tactics and its millennialist views ... Reader's conclusions, which are clearly analyzed throughout his text, are the most reasoned of any explanation of what Aum is all about. The other works under review here fail to approach his scholarly analysis and in-depth research.

– Japanese Journal of Religious Studies (vol. 24, nos 1–2, 1997)

The Nordic Institute of Asian Studies (NIAS) is funded by the governments of Denmark, Finland, Iceland, Norway and Sweden via the Nordic Council of Ministers, and works to encourage and support Asian studies in the Nordic countries. In so doing, NIAS has published well in excess of one hundred books in the last three decades, most of them in co-operation with Curzon Press.

Nordic Council of Ministers